MASTERS AT WORK

MASTERS AT WORK

BECOMING A NEUROSURGEON

JOHN COLAPINTO

SIMON & SCHUSTER

New York   London   Toronto   Sydney   New Delhi

Simon & Schuster
1230 Avenue of the Americas
New York, NY 10020

Copyright © 2019 by Simon & Schuster, Inc.

All rights reserved, including the right to reproduce this book
or portions thereof in any form whatsoever. For information, address
Simon & Schuster Subsidiary Rights Department,
1230 Avenue of the Americas, New York, NY 10020.

Certain names have been changed, including those of all patients,
as have certain identifying characteristics.

First Simon & Schuster hardcover edition April 2019

SIMON & SCHUSTER and colophon are registered trademarks
of Simon & Schuster, Inc.

For information about special discounts for bulk purchases,
please contact Simon & Schuster Special Sales at 1-866-506-1949
or business@simonandschuster.com.

The Simon & Schuster Speakers Bureau can bring authors to your
live event. For more information, or to book an event, contact
the Simon & Schuster Speakers Bureau at 1-866-248-3049
or visit our website at www.simonspeakers.com.

Illustrations by Donna Mehalko

Manufactured in the United States of America

1   3   5   7   9   10   8   6   4   2

Library of Congress Cataloging-in-Publication Data

Names: Colapinto, John [date], author.
Title: Becoming a neurosurgeon / John Colapinto.
Description: New York : Simon & Schuster, [2018] | Series: Masters at work
Identifiers: LCCN 2017022619| ISBN 9781501159176 (hardcover) | ISBN
9781501159190 (e-book) | ISBN 9781501159183 (trade paperback) Subjects: LCSH:
Nervous system—Surgery. | Neurosurgeons—Training of.
Classification: LCC RD593 .C592 2018 | DDC 617.4/80076—dc23

LC record available at https://lccn.loc.gov/2017022619

ISBN 978-1-5011-5917-6
ISBN 978-1-5011-5919-0 (ebook)

To Donna and Johnny

CONTENTS

BECOMING A
NEUROSURGEON

_____

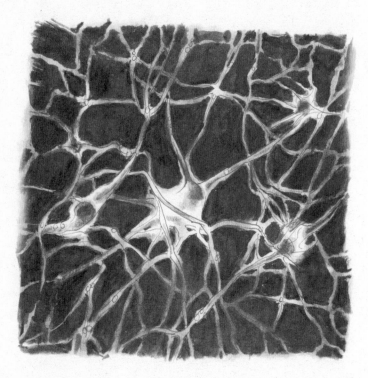

Neurons

1

t is 8:33 a.m. and Dr. Amir Madani, a neurosurgery resident at Mount Sinai, the large teaching hospital on Manhattan's Upper East Side, is about to perform the final operation in his training as a brain surgeon. A team of doctors and nurses, eight people in all, dressed in blue scrubs and white paper face masks, move around Operating Room #2, preparing equipment, as the patient, a forty-year-old African-American woman, is wheeled in on a gurney. She is transferred onto an operating table in the center of the room, and the anesthesiologist inserts an IV needle into her right arm. He begins a drip of propofol, a powerful sedative. Within seconds, she is unconscious. A nurse, standing between the patient's legs, places a catheter to drain urine during what is expected to be a four-hour-long operation. The scrub nurse arranges instruments—scalpels, forceps, sponges—on a large table beside the bed. Once all is in readiness, the neurosurgery resident, Dr. Madani, a tall, sad-eyed man in his late thirties, ties a surgical mask over his face and steps over to the sleeping patient.

"Okay," he says, "let's do this."

Neurosurgery residency, the training period for brain surgeons after their four years of medical school, is the most grueling in all of medicine. Trainees work upward of 120 hours a week, often on as little as one or two hours of sleep a night. They do this for seven years, the longest of any surgical specialty. This will be Madani's 1,807th operation at Mount Sinai, and his 180th assisting Dr. Joshua Bederson, the chairman of the department of neurosurgery.

It is a remarkable case on which to be going out. The patient had been in an accident six months earlier, hit in her car by a pickup that tried to swerve around her at a red light. A minor case of whiplash prompted a CT scan of her head and neck—which revealed, serendipitously, a massive brain tumor the size of a man's fist in her left frontal lobe, just above the eye. The tumor's spherical, self-contained shape suggested that it was of a slow-growing type that had, in all likelihood, been expanding for decades. The tumor now threatened to crowd out the healthy tissues (which have little room to expand within the closed box of the skull), inducing swelling that could cause her brain, squeezed like toothpaste in a tube, to "herniate"—to push out through the hole where her skull joins the spine. This would crush the brain stem, the seat of such vital functions as breathing and heartbeat—instantly killing her.

Three months ago, in early March, Bederson, with Madani assisting, had eliminated the immediate danger to the patient by opening her skull, cutting a tiny two-centimeter slit in the surface of the brain, and decompressing the tumor by draining it of a watery yellow liquid that had been building up. They then removed the growth. Such tumors, however, are encapsulated in a thin skin or rind. The patient was now scheduled to have that rind removed, since a biopsy showed that it contained pre-cancerous cells.

The patient had, in the meantime, undergone a complete transformation. For her entire adult life, she had been anti-social, depressed, lethargic, spending the better part of the previous twenty-three years on the sofa watching television. In the months since that first operation, she had begun rising early to exercise and had shed fifty pounds. She now took intense pleasure in every aspect of her life—especially her two children, seventeen and fourteen years old, for whom she had performed parental duties like preparing meals but from whom she had been emotionally isolated and distant. She could now barely restrain herself from constantly kissing and touching them, as if discovering them for the first time. She felt the same way about her husband. They had met when she was eighteen years old and fallen in love, but she had shown little real affection toward him since 1996, when they married.

Neurosurgeons have long known about the changes in mood and personality that can take place through manipulation of the frontal lobes, but rarely does a patient show so dramatic a change in temperament and outlook as had occurred in this case—especially so soon after treatment. While coming out of the anesthetic after the initial operation, she began laughing and pointing at the anesthetist and loudly, playfully proclaiming, "I know you! I know you!" The surgical staff dubbed her "The Giggler" because of her infectious, easily triggered laugh. At the time of her second surgery, to remove the tumor lining, she was making plans to enroll in nursing school. She had given up coffee, after a decades-long "addiction," and wine. She no longer watched TV—too busy exercising, talking, reading, *living*. Old texts on her smartphone—messages filled with bitterness, despair, and deep pessimism—mystified her. "I don't know who that person is," she said, before going into the second operation. "I know it was me, but it doesn't seem possible."

IN THE OPERATING ROOM Madani tapes a pair of latex-free plastic strips over the patient's eyes. He talks as he works. "There is a fascinating account of frontal lobe surgery in

Penfield's letters," he says, referring to Wilder Penfield, the early-twentieth-century physician recognized to be one of the grandfathers of modern neurosurgery. "In the late 1920s, he operated on his sister and removed a frontal lobe tumor. After doing the routine post-op tests in the hospital, he said, 'Oh she's doing really well.' But later, he was at her house and saw that the place was incredibly messy, she couldn't manage two things at a time. She was confused, disoriented. She'd always been meticulously organized. He realized that the frontal lobe is extremely important, but mysterious. Almost a century later, we're still so ignorant about what the frontal lobe *does*—or how it does it."

The same could be said for the brain as a whole: a three-pound lump of jelly-like matter whose hundred billion cells, and the trillions of electrochemical connections between them, make up the most complex system in the known universe. This system is responsible not only for all motor and sensory functions of the body but for the mystery of consciousness itself and all to which it gives rise: love, hope, memory, fear, music, poetry, art, science—everything, in short, that makes us human. That so little is known about the anatomy and functioning of the brain is one reason neurosurgery is so demanding and so dangerous. Those who expose and cut into the brain's tissues are, to a very real degree, traveling in terra incognita. Indeed, so fraught with risk is opening the skull and invading the brain—where a millimeter's error can spell disaster—no reasonable medical professional would perform these interventions save for the fact that patients who end up in neurosurgery wards are already suffering from calamities so threatening to their life and well-being that nonintervention is not an option.

"With this patient," Madani goes on, gesturing at the woman on the table, "there was a *huge* mass that we decompressed in her frontal lobe. So the pressure of that tumor was affecting the neuronal communication in a very complex way, and it altered her personality. But how? Who knows? Was the tumor suppressing the electrical activity of the cells by squashing the frontal lobe against the inside of the skull? Maybe. Or maybe the tumor was secreting some chemical agents that interfere. On a molecular level there is so much going on that we cannot see with our imaging tools—and that we'll maybe never know."

He wields a hairbrush to make a part in the patient's hair, exposing a long thin scar from the earlier operation. The scar arcs over the top of her head from temple to temple, about an inch behind the hairline. As he works, he says, wistfully, "This is the last time I'll do this at Mount Sinai."

A nurse, who sits in a corner monitoring the patient's brain activity on a computer, asks what he plans to do next.

"Me?" Madani deadpans, as he brushes an antiseptic gel

into the patient's hair. "I'll be opening a barbershop. Doing similar stuff, just slightly less stressful." Laughter fills the room.

"No," he continues, "I'm going to spend two years in Toronto doing a fellowship in deep brain stimulation." (DBS involves inserting electrodes into the brain to stimulate areas associated with movement disorders like Parkinson's Disease and mood disorders like depression.) "That means," Madani says, "that, by the time I finish my neurosurgical education, I will have been in school for *twenty-one* years after high school." This includes four years pre-med in math and biochemistry at Columbia University, eight years of medical school to obtain a combined MD and PhD at SUNY Downstate in Brooklyn, his seven years of residency at Mount Sinai, and the two-year plan for a fellowship in Toronto. "Neurosurgery is the only profession where you've started to have arteriosclerosis before you finish your training."

Madani wields a huge metal clamp, a medieval-looking instrument, with a set of dagger-like points aiming inward. This is a so-called Mayfield device, named after its creator, Dr. Frank H. Mayfield, who made the first prototype in the late 1960s. It is used to hold the patient's head completely still during the surgery. He positions the points over her temples, taking care not to puncture the band of muscles that encircles this part of the head—to do so would allow her head to shift, disastrously, during the operation. He pushes the clamp together, the points penetrating the skin and touching the bone of the skull. With her head now clamped in the vise jaws, he secures the long extension arm of the Mayfield to the bottom of the bed and tightens the bolt.

"But I can't complain," he goes on. "I wanted to do this, and nothing but this, since I was a teenager." He'd become fascinated with the brain in high school when he saw a TV documentary about Nobel Prize winner Santiago Ramón y Cajal, a Spanish pathologist who, in the early 1900s, perfected the means for staining brain cells. This was a groundbreaking leap: It allowed scientists to define the precise structure of neurons—the central cell body and nucleus, the spidery dendrites and long tail-like axon—and to draw the first blueprint for how these neurons communicate with each other through chemical and electrical impulses that leap across the tiny gap, called a synapse, between them. "I just fell in love with the brain," Madani says.

Many neurosurgeons are highly competitive super-achievers: college athletic champions and Eagle scouts, people driven to take on the most difficult challenges. Madani professes not to be one of those. "I have no other talents or skills," he says. "This is all I ever wanted. So it's actually a little scary to think what would have happened if I had not made it into the program."

The odds of not making it were high. Mount Sinai's neurosurgery residency program received applications from more than three hundred medical students this year. It chose two.

Present in the OR is a third-year medical student, Rui Feng, a slightly built young woman in her midtwenties. She hopes, one day, to be one of those chosen for the program. Like Madani, Rui is single-minded about neurosurgery. "It's all I want, too," she tells him. Her chances of making it seem good. Dr. Bederson, the chief of the department, has recently awarded her a full paid fellowship to do a scholarly year in neurosurgery—one of only two or three such scholarships he awards each year. ("She is destined to be a star," Bederson says. "If she could sit on my shoulder all day long, she'd do it.") As a medical student, Rui's participation in operations, apart from rudimentary actions like using a suction tool to suck blood from a scalp incision as it is being cut, is purely that of an observer. But her appetite for such observation is insatiable. She tells Madani: "A couple of days ago I watched Dr. Yong"—one of Mount Sinai's full-time attending neurosurgeons—"do a fourteen-hour surgery to remove a tumor. When they got the scans back they realized they didn't get all of it, so they went back in and operated for another eight hours. Those are my favorites."

"It's insane, what you guys do," says the anesthesiologist, from his position at the foot of the bed, where he will monitor the patient's vital functions—respiration, heart rate—during the operation. "Actually, I know three different guys—all from Johns Hopkins—who burned out during their neurosurgical residencies. The first guy, he was in, like, year four, and he quit and joined the military—he's now in the infantry in Iraq."

"What?" says Madani, incredulous. "Did they scan his head? He might have had a frontal lobe tumor."

Madani and Rui place long wedges of foam rubber under the patient's arms, then secure her to the table with a series of seatbelt-like straps that they pull tight over her upper body. They cover her, head to toe, in blue paper drapes, one of which has a small clear plastic window pre-cut to expose only the area on her head where they will be operating.

At 9:26 a.m., Madani is ready to "open"—the term used to describe the surgical penetration of the scalp and skull to expose the brain. Conversation ceases as he takes up a cauterizing needle, a thin blade with an electrically charged tip that simultaneously seals blood vessels with heat as it cuts. He places the tip against the scar that arcs across the upper part of the woman's forehead and begins to slice. A wisp of smoke rises from the incision and an aroma of seared flesh fills the room. Rui plies the suction tool, a small hollow wand, to suck away the small trickle of blood that seeps from the wound. Madani proceeds slowly, carefully. Once he's made the long cut from ear to ear, he works his fingertips under the front edge of the flap of skin and muscle and tries to tug it forward over her face. The scalp clings stubbornly to the skull. He uses a flat-ended metal tool and works it under the scalp, like a man using a spatula to free up eggs stuck to a pan. Again using his fingers, he slowly peels the flap up and pulls it over the patient's face, exposing a large portion of skull, from hairline to eyebrow ridge. The curved expanse of bone is thickly smeared with blood.

Ordinarily, to open the bone, Madani would use a small handheld instrument that looks like a dentist's drill, cutting a window of a few inches square. That won't be necessary today. They'll go in through the opening they made three months before when they decompressed the tumor. That opening is clearly visible, the so-called "bone flap" screwed down with four titanium clips known as "snowflake" clips because of their irregular but symmetrical shape, which indeed resemble snowflakes. Madani uses a screwdriver to loosen the screws, removes the clips and lifts off the skull flap, a slightly curved piece of bone about two inches by

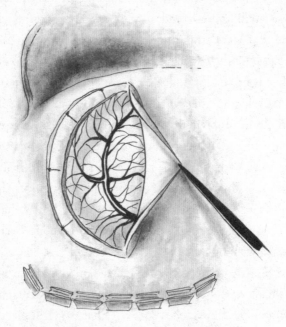

Pulling back the dura to expose the cortical surface

three inches in dimension. He hands it to the scrub nurse, who places it in a shallow container on a nearby table.

Madani has one more layer to get through to expose the brain's surface: a thin, tough protective covering, called the dura, which has a bright silvery look, like a piece of synthetic fabric. It carries a U-shaped scar from the previous operation, but Madani will enter with a new incision—a linear cut down the center. Working slowly with scalpel and miniature scissors (". . . don't want to injure any of those cortical veins . . ." he mutters as he works), he makes a vertical cut of two inches. With a pair of forceps, he delicately grasps the edges of the dura and pulls it back to reveal the surface of the brain. It is shiny pinkish-white with a pearly sheen, its thick ridges and folds of cortical tissue glistening, the surface crisscrossed with an intricate network of bright red arteries and thick blue-green veins. It lightly pulses in time with the patient's heartbeat. Madani has seen this countless times, but the sight never fails to evoke awe. "Amazing to think that that blobby matter is everything that makes us *us*," he says.

A couple of nurses roll the intra-operative microscope into place. It's a large piece of equipment, seven feet in height, on a wheeled base with an arcing, cantilevered arm that, at one end, holds a 150-pound microscope outfitted with a pair of stereoscopic magnifying lenses and a set of handgrips.

Madani sits on a specially designed ergonomic operating chair, which looks like a dentist's chair, behind the patient's head and aims the microscope at the opening in the skull. Through the eyepieces, his view is breathtaking. Like a vast alpine range viewed from a low-flying plane, a three-dimensional panorama on which the tiniest structures—squiggly hair-thin capillaries on the cortical surface—appear as clearly as a system of interconnected mountain roads.

The scrub nurse hands Madani a pair of forceps.

To the patient's left is the so-called "Brain Lab"—a set of computer consoles with screens that project CT and MRI scans made of the patient's head the night before. An infrared camera at the foot of the bed will track the movement of the surgical instruments, like a kind of Google Maps for the human body, projecting the instruments' location inside the scan of the patient's brain, helping the surgeons to precisely target the tumor and avoid dangerous areas of so-called "eloquent" brain—those regions responsible for higher "executive" functions such as thought, speech, memory.

With a retractor—a broad curved tool—in his opposite hand, Madani gingerly pulls to one side healthy brain tissue and exposes part of the pre-cancerous lining that is to be removed. A yellow substance, resembling chicken fat, the tumor capsule is quite different in color and texture from the healthy parts of the brain. Probing deeper, he uncovers a shiny bluish structure behind the pearly jelly. This is the left ventricle, one of the four balloon-like cavities in the center of the brain that generate cerebrospinal fluid, the clear liquid in which the brain effectively floats within the skull and that provides a natural shock absorber for the cortex and spinal cord.

Madani lifts the instruments from the patient's head.

As one of three chief residents at Mount Sinai, Madani is

entrusted with opening and closing the skull. But the bulk of the neurosurgical operations performed in any teaching hospital are the responsibility of full-time attending surgeons from whom the residents learn by up-close observation.

Madani sits back and says, "Okay, we're ready for Dr. Bederson."

2

At 10:35 a.m., Bederson arrives in the operating room. He is, at fifty-nine years old, a man of medium height with a powerful, well-knit physique. A former college gymnastics champion, he still runs several miles a day and does regular push-ups and sit-ups. His chiseled face and bald head give him an aura of monkish austerity, and an unusual physiological quirk lends his gaze a special intensity: His irises are the same color as his pupils, making his eyes appear like two depthless black pools—coincidentally, an effect shared by one of Bederson's idols, Pablo Picasso.

As chief of the department, Bederson is responsible for guiding the activities of his thirty attending neurosurgeons and fourteen residents, steering research, setting long-term goals for growth, hiring and firing, but he also likes to keep his hand in as a surgeon, and he performs between 120 and 130 procedures a year, some two or three a week. In ordinary life, he is friendly, talkative, and warm. But the operating room is not ordinary life. It is a high-stakes arena where he must set an example of supreme focus and seriousness for his trainees—as well as himself. He forbids all music in the OR and discourages excessive talking, even for procedures like this one, which, for someone of his experience, is routine. Except that no craniotomy—the technical term for an operation that involves opening the skull—is routine.

"So, how's it going?" he asks, as he ties on a surgical mask.

"We are much closer to the ventricle than we thought," Madani says.

Bederson sits on the operating chair that Madani has vacated and places his forearms on a padded armrest in front of him. The nurse hands him a pair of cauterizing forceps, a tool that permits him to not only grasp pieces of brain but also to administer small bursts of heat through the tips of the forceps in order to stop any bleeding that might result from manipulation of the infinitely delicate tissues. In his left hand, Bederson takes up a suction tool. For surgeries anywhere else in the body, the scalpel is the surgeon's most important tool for the removal of diseased or damaged tissue, which is cut away with the blade. It is a measure of the supreme delicacy of the brain that the neurosurgeon's most important piece of equipment is the suction tool, whose gentle sucking power permits a less aggressive and invasive means of carefully coaxing diseased tissue from healthy brain.

Looking down the scope and feeling around gently with the tips of his forceps, Bederson stakes out the margins of the tumor lining. With the suction tool, he gently sucks at the diseased tissue, taking care not to tear the healthy tissues to which the tumor lining stickily adheres. He works swiftly but never hastily: Neurosurgery is an art of small, infinitely judicious movements. "You have the physical problem of the brain tissue being very soft and really not resistant at all to manipulation," Bederson says later, in describing one of the factors that makes neurosurgery so demanding. "Heart surgeons have a lot of training and it's very difficult, but the blood vessels of the heart—and the heart itself—are really tough and resilient, and they're easy to work with. You grab them and you move them around. They take a joke. Brain tissue does not."

Bederson is known among residents, colleagues, and mentors as one of the finest technical surgeons in the world. This is owing, in part, to his innately superior hand-eye coordination and three-dimensional spatial understanding. He was in second grade when his mother, recognizing his love for making things with his hands, first enrolled him in a sculpture class. He continued to sculpt through high school and university and is rare—perhaps unique—in neurosurgery for having taken a year off between his second and third years of medical school to study sculpture, at New

York University, earning a master of fine arts degree, before returning to medical school. He remains a dedicated sculptor, working on large and small pieces, in a variety of mediums, in his home studio adjoining his house in Briarcliff Manor, north of New York City. He says that the connection between sculpture and neurosurgery is obvious. "If it's my intention to sculpt a hand from a block of marble," he says, "I see the hand inside the block, which takes a degree of 3-D spatial reasoning and understanding of anatomy. To liberate that hand, you've got to remove everything that is not relevant to the hand. Removing a tumor from around blood vessels and fragile nerves is almost the same. You go through that tumor to reveal the normal, beautiful anatomy inside."

Bederson's surgical expertise is also owing to the eight years he spent training under three legendary neurosurgeons of the last century—Charles Wilson in San Francisco, Gazi Yaşargil in Switzerland, and Robert Spetzler in Phoenix—all of whom are recognized as the finest technical surgeons the specialty has ever produced and inventors of many of the procedures used in neurosurgical operating rooms around the world today. All of this has aided Bederson in integrating the second-to-second judgments and risk assessments of neurosurgery with the complex physical coordination demanded by the specialty. A pedal under his left foot allows him to zoom and pan with the microscope without using his hands. A pedal under his right foot passes electric current between the tips of the cautery forceps in his right hand. Over time, the coordinated use of the pedals, the microscope, and the tools has become second nature—"integrated into the cerebellum," as Bederson puts it. But this did not happen overnight. "For the longest time," he now tells Madani, "I couldn't do this and talk. It was as if all my mental resources were focused on my hands and I didn't even want to ask for an instrument. But then I realized that I *have* to talk—because people can't read my mind."

He works, sucking away at the tumor capsule, collapsing it away from the healthy brain, while Madani, standing beside him, watches intently through a second set of observer's eyepieces. After a few minutes, Bederson asks Madani to let Rui, the medical student, have a look. She steps over to the scope and peers into the eyepieces.

"I just passed through an open space," Bederson says. "Where do you think we are?"

It's a tough question to put to a third-year med student, given the immense complexity of the brain's anatomy, which can be bewildering even to experienced residents, who have been witnessing operations for four, five, six years. Through the microscope, the various landmarks are not clearly demarcated and color-coded as in the textbooks, but appear instead as an indeterminate mass of pearly jelly, spidering nerves, and branching blood vessels—all of it awash in cerebrospinal fluid and blood. But this is precisely why Rui loves observing actual operations. "It's really the *only* way to learn," she says later. "To follow which direction is which, and which tissue is which, and what they're trying to avoid."

Peering into the microscope, she thinks for a while. After a moment, she says, "Sagittal sinus?"

"Very good," Bederson says. He adds, "Not the sagittal sinus itself but the . . . ?"

She ponders for a second. "The Falx?"

"Good for you," he says. "The medial surface of the right frontal lobe."

Bederson himself is recognized among his colleagues and residents for rarely, if ever, becoming disoriented within the complicated labyrinth of the brain, for always knowing where he is, spatially, and this, too, might be owing to certain innate abilities. His high-school gymnastics coach, Tom Auchterlonie, says that Bederson was the best gymnast he ever trained and that this was owing to a particular faculty shared by only the most gifted in the sport. "In gymnastics we have something called 'conscious proprioception,'" Auchterlonie says. "Knowing where you are in space. Josh knew *exactly* where he was in space, twisting or turning, or spinning upside down, at all times. A lot of the very best gymnasts have that; and those that don't do not progress too far, because when you're on the high bar, eight feet off the ground—and by the time you leave the bar you're sometimes *twelve* feet off the ground—you'd *better* know where you are because you're not falling into water, you're falling onto the floor."

"Okay," Bederson says to Rui. "Let Amir back in."

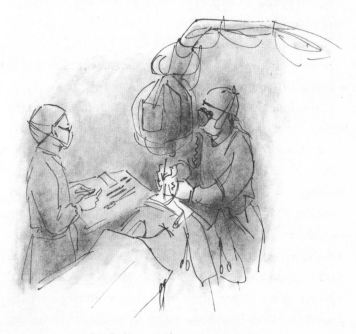

Dr. Bederson performing a craniotomy

Rui steps away from the microscope and Madani moves back into place.

As a physician who trains neurosurgeons, Bederson must judge the skill level and competence of his residents to decide when it is opportune—and safe—to hand them the reins in an operation and allow them to remove tumor.

Only chief residents, those in their sixth and seventh years, are afforded this chance. Bederson now asks Madani to take over for a while. "I've defined the margins," he says. "Call me when you're ready."

Bederson leaves the OR and heads to his office.

Madani sits and, with his forceps, begins carefully lifting out bits of the tumor.

"Specimen," he says, holding out a lump of tissue to the scrub nurse, who uses his gloved fingers to pull the sticky mass off the forceps. He places the piece of tumor in a cup.

The specimen is immediately taken upstairs to the pathology lab, where it is put under a quick analysis to determine what kind of cancer cells it contains. Such instant results are known as a "frozen." More detailed analysis, which can take a week, is called a "permanent." Madani works for another twenty minutes, removing tumor, until a phone in the corner of the operating room rings. It's the pathology lab calling down with the results of the frozen.

Madani takes it, listens for a moment, then announces to the room: "Low-grade tumor."

Although brain tumors are colloquially referred to as benign or malignant, this is a misnomer. All brain tumors fall on a spectrum from not very cancerous (that is, low-grade, slow-growing, "benign" tumors), to highly cancerous (that is, high-grade, furiously aggressive, fast-growing "malignant" tumors), and through every shade in between. That this patient's tumor is low grade—slow growing and noninvasive—suggests to Madani that they do not need to risk being superaggressive in removing every last cell. A certain part of the tumor, near the top of the brain, is perilously close to a critical language area—a single false move could destroy the patient's ability to speak or understand words. Perhaps it would be best to leave it and monitor any possible regrowth with regular brain scans? Much of neurosurgery is knowing when to leave well enough alone.

He pokes carefully at the bolus of brownish gray tissue. He admits that he's not sure whether it is tumor or simply gray matter that has been discolored by heat from the cautery forceps. "I don't think it's tumor," he says in a noncommittal voice. "Can someone call Bederson?"

At 12:09 p.m., Bederson reappears in the OR and settles into the operating chair.

"The frozen came back low grade," Madani says. "I don't think we need to be very aggressive."

"Why did you leave this bit here?" Bederson immediately asks, pointing with his forceps at the discolored tissue near the surface of the brain. Madani confesses that he was not sure if it was tumor—and that he didn't want to risk taking it out because of its dangerous location.

"There's tumor in it," Bederson says. He feels the mass with his forceps, lightly pinching it. "That is tumor until proven otherwise. It's gelatinous," he adds, referring to the gumminess he can detect through the tips of his forceps, which adhere slightly to the tissue. Such stickiness is, to experienced surgeons like Bederson, a red flag. "We have to assume it's tumor." He begins to suck it off the healthy tissue—efficiently, swiftly, but precisely. What, for Madani, would have been a highly challenging, and risky, technical maneuver is, for someone of Bederson's skill and experience, almost easy. As he works, Bederson falls into a conversational mood, rare for him in the OR—perhaps inspired by his knowledge that this is Madani's final day at Mount Sinai, their last operation together.

"What is it that experience teaches us about doing surgeries?" Bederson asks. "If you had to summarize? How has experience changed you as a neurosurgeon?"

"It's hard to say," Madani says, as he peers down the

scope, watching Bederson's masterful manipulation of the instruments and tissues. "What I'm really concentrated on these days . . ." He pauses, then resumes on a new tack—clearly thinking about the caution that had prevented him from attacking the top of the tumor. "I don't know at what point I might cause more damage. By seeing more cases I have a better understanding of the very detailed anatomy, and so I can avoid doing something dangerous."

"But it's more than that, isn't it?" Bederson counters. "Because it can also be more dangerous *not* to operate. With experience, you learn how to do things. Then you learn what you *can* do, what you are able to accomplish. You also learn what you *cannot* do. And then hopefully you learn what you *should* do."

"I think it's important to know your limits," Madani says, as if tacitly defending his decision to not be too aggressive with this tumor. "What if some complication happens?"

Complication is the surgical euphemism for those physician errors that lead to disastrous results for patients, including permanent disability or death.

"This gets to the question of ability and confidence," Bederson says. "Let's say someone had an *ability* that's very low—call it one on a scale of one to three. But he has a *confidence* that's very high—a three. He'd be the most dangerous neurosurgeon on the planet. But someone with a very low confidence level of one and a very high ability of three is an *ineffective* surgeon. So you want, as much as possible, a match between confidence and ability."

In describing the neurosurgeon whose high confidence matches his high ability, Bederson has, in effect, described the kind of neurosurgeon that he has, over the last twenty-five years, become: a physician whose technical expertise is matched by a confidence that, in someone less technically adept, could be judged almost too high. A self-described risk taker by temperament, his hobbies over the years have included mountain climbing, hang gliding, motorcycle riding, and piloting a small plane. As a sophomore, he once used his free-style rock-climbing skills to scale the four-story tower of his high school in Mamaroneck, New York, using only the tiny finger grips between the bricks—a stunt that, today, he admits was "incredibly stupid." At the same time, he says that the feat suggested certain traits typical of many who pursue neurosurgery. "I mean," he says, "I did write my initials—JB—at the top."

He operates for a few more minutes, then he lifts his instruments from the woman's head and stands. "Okay. I think I got everything. You can close." He leaves the room.

The patient's brain now has a hole in it about the circumference of a silver dollar and an inch deep. Brain tissue cannot regrow, but the hole will later well up with cerebrospinal fluid and the tissues will expand to fill in the gap on their own. Instead of trying to close the delicate dura, Madani sews in a patch of AlloDerm, a membrane harvested, as he puts it, from "the skin of people no longer with us." He lays on shiny wafer-thin pieces of oxidized cellulose, a water-insoluble compound that acts as an antihemorrhagic, to prevent bleeding. (A bleed between the skull and brain, known as a subdural hematoma, is one of the major complications of neurosurgery and can be fatal.) He puts in a layer of gel foam, a coagulant, to further discourage bleeding and, like a man fitting the final piece into a jigsaw puzzle, replaces the bone flap. He screws down the snowflake clips. "This is going to be on her forehead, so we want to get these screws nice and flush. Otherwise you're going to see it through the skin." He rolls the scalp back over her skull. "Crazy, huh?" he says.

Using two pairs of forceps, with which he manipulates the needle and thread, he begins to sew the scalp closed with exceptional dexterity and speed. Earlier in his training, Madani worked in electron microscopy, investigating cells at a molecular level of magnification, where he had to use forceps to manipulate slices of membrane cut to a thickness of 5 nanometers. "My favorite part is sewing up," he says. "I could use staples, but I don't like to. I like to do it perfectly."

As he sews, Madani talks about the ease with which

Bederson removed the final bits of tumor. "It's largely a *feel* thing, the texture of the tissues through the forceps," he says. "That comes with experience. And I don't mean seven years of residency. I mean a lifetime." Indeed, Madani says, even after assisting on over 1,800 brain surgeries, he still feels like a neophyte next to Bederson. "It's not like now that I'm graduating, I'm going to do perfect surgeries. They say it's ten years learning, post-residency, until you reach your plateau. And hopefully your plateau is that you end up as a very good surgeon."

Few, he says, become great, like Bederson.

"He's really one of the best you'll ever see," Madani says. "It's like when you talk about a great painter. The fluidity of his hand movements. The ease throughout his whole body. He's not somebody who's *trying hard* during surgery. He's sitting comfortably, he's not contorted and saying 'Oh it's not working'—everything is beautiful and relaxed. You don't see that in anybody else. You don't see that elegance."

He rolls gauze around the patient's head, circling the brow several times, then wrapping it under her chin, pulling the bandage tight, to discourage bleeding under the scalp. It's 2:15 p.m. The operation took just under five hours—short, by neurosurgery standards.

Dr. Lee, the anesthesiologist, introduces a chemical into the IV drip to bring the patient back to consciousness. He steps to the side of the bed and removes the tape from her closed eyelids, which suddenly twitch. That the patient should be surfacing into consciousness mere seconds after the controlled violence done to her head seems almost inconceivable, a kind of miracle.

"Big, deep breath!" Lee shouts, as if trying to make himself heard by someone at a great distance. "Deep breath!"

The patient inhales—and Dr. Lee quickly slides out the respirator tube that has been down her throat.

Madani leans over the bed. "Can you show me two fingers?" he says.

She groggily raises a hand, two fingers extended. He asks her to do it with her other hand. She does.

"It's working!" Madani says, with unfeigned joy and relief. "We rebooted!"

3

The earliest known neurosurgical procedure, called "trepanation"—the chiseling of holes in the skull, presumably to relieve pressure on the brain but possibly also for spiritual reasons—dates to prehistory; specifically the Neolithic period, which began around 10,000 BC and ended in 4500 BC. Cave paintings depict the procedure, and ancient skull remains show signs of healing from the operation, which suggest that some patients actually survived it. Fossil evidence of trepanation has been found at archeological sites around the world, including in China, Russia, Europe, and Mesoamerica. The Greek physician Galen, in the last half of the second century AD, mentioned the procedure in a treatise on the brain. Galen recommended that once the skull had been opened, physicians put something, like a piece of fabric, against the exposed cortex to protect it from injury—although, he warned, if this protective layer were "pressed too heavily . . . the effect is to render the person senseless as well as incapable of all voluntary motion."

In the centuries after Galen, scientists made considerable strides in describing the anatomy and functioning of the brain—usually through animal experiments and autopsies of people who had died from brain illnesses or injuries. The electrical basis of cellular communication in the brain and nervous system was discovered in experiments (a century before Edison's pioneering breakthroughs in electricity) by the Italian researcher Luigi Galvani. In 1791, Galvani published papers describing how a static electrical spark applied to the nerves of a dead frog caused the animal's legs to twitch. In 1848, a railroad worker in New England, Phineas Gage, became a famous patient in neuroscience when an on-the-job explosion drove an iron rod up through his jaw and out the top of his head; miraculously, he survived, but friends and family noted the dramatic change in his temperament when the formerly quiet and polite Gage began swearing and acting with impulsive childishness—which suggested the role of the frontal lobes in regulating mood and behavior. Then, in the early 1860s, Paul Broca, a French physician, after studying multiple autopsy results on patients who had lost the ability to speak after stroke or head injury, discovered that each had suffered damage to a very specific part of the brain, in the left frontal area of the cerebral cortex—above the left eye and a few inches back—a speech region now known as Broca's Area. This was the first definitive proof of "cortical localization": the idea that very specific regions of the brain control very particular functions of the body—a breakthrough that had decisive implications for the practice of neurosurgery.

Indeed, until Broca's discovery, brain surgery had not progressed much beyond trepanation, as described by Galen seventeen centuries earlier. The problem was that accurately diagnosing and treating brain lesions (tumors, blood clots, aneurysms, abscesses) in living patients was next to impossible given the inability of doctors to see inside the skull. Broca's insights into how particular brain areas control specific functions allowed surgeons to deduce the location of lesions according to the clinical symptoms presented by a patient. This allowed a Scottish surgeon named William Macewen, in 1879, to perform the first neurosurgical removal of a brain tumor, when a teenaged girl was brought to him suffering from seizures of the right arm and face. Because Macewen knew that the spasms of this patient's forelimbs and face were controlled by a specific area of the brain (located on the opposite side from the affected body parts, since researchers had by then established that the left side of the body is controlled by the right hemisphere of the brain, the right side of the body by the left hemisphere), he was able to infer the location of the lesion. He duly opened her skull and found and removed a tumor. The girl lived. Macewen went on to diagnose and surgically treat various brain lesions, and he published his results.

But few surgeons (or patients) were willing to follow Macewen's lead because of the exceptionally high mortality rate for such surgeries experienced by Macewen and the small number of doctors willing to adopt his methods. Greater than 60 percent of such patients did not survive, which prompted one writer to say that those who underwent Macewen's pioneering form of brain surgery faced a "near-certain death sentence."

Survival odds improved dramatically in the early twentieth century through the efforts of the doctor who is today known as the founder of modern neurosurgery, Harvey Cushing. Born in Cleveland, Ohio, in 1869, Cushing graduated from Harvard Medical School and by 1905 had established himself as the first surgeon in the United States to dedicate himself exclusively to brain surgery. Practicing at Johns Hopkins Hospital in Baltimore and later at Harvard's Peter Bent Brigham Hospital, Cushing introduced a number of refinements and innovations that reduced the mortality rate for neurosurgery to below 10 percent. With the Harvard physicist William T. Bovie, he developed the cautery device that enables coagulation of the blood vessels when cutting into brain tissue or tumors, a critical tool that reduces the likelihood of the uncontrolled hemorrhages that, until then, were a major cause of death through patients bleeding out on the table. (Mental activity requires immense amounts of blood: a quarter of the blood pumped from the heart circulates through the brain.) Cushing also introduced new means for monitoring and regulating blood pressure during surgery, making possible treatment for conditions previously considered inoperable, including subdural hematomas in newborns (which can result from injury to the child's head from the improper use of birthing tools, maternal alcohol abuse, or even the mother's excessive use of blood-thinning agents, like aspirin, while pregnant). Cushing developed pioneering methods for operating on the pituitary gland, often called the body's "master gland," crucial for many bodily functions, including the control of hormones implicated in body growth, the onset of puberty, and the secretion of adrenaline. A pea-sized organ located in a difficult-to-reach area deep in the center of the brain, in a bony cavity right behind the nose, the pituitary had eluded surgical manipulation. But Cushing showed how the gland could be reached with no damage to a healthy brain if the surgeon went in through the patient's nostril, broke through the thin layer of bone at the back of the nasal cavity, and reached through the so-called sphenoidal sinus, the narrow gap that separates the right and left hemispheres of the brain. He also performed one of the first successful operations for trigeminal neuralgia, an excruciating facial pain that results from blood vessels pressing against nerves in the face.

Cushing published widely about his positive outcomes,

thereby drawing patients from around the world to his clinics. He also created the first academic neurosurgery department, at Harvard, and trained generations of neurosurgical residents who would carry on his techniques, versions of which are still in practice in operating rooms today. By the time of his retirement in 1937, and his death two years later, Cushing had transformed neurosurgery from a fringe therapy practiced by only a handful of especially fearless surgeons, like Macewen, into a highly professionalized medical specialty.

The essential techniques of neurosurgery pioneered and perfected by Cushing remained little changed for almost three decades after his death—until the mid-1960s and the advent of the intra-operative microscope. Originally developed for gynecological procedures, the microscope was soon adopted by throat surgeons to peer into previously obscure regions of the larynx for operation on the vocal cords. One of the first to take up the microscope for use in neurosurgery, in 1961, was the Turkish-born physician Gazi Yaşargil, an attending surgeon at the Zurich University Hospital in Switzerland. Yaşargil, who was born in 1925, is today, at age ninety-one, recognized as the single greatest creative genius of late twentieth-century neurosurgery. He ignored the initial derision and disbelief of colleagues and extolled the virtues of greater visibility afforded by the microscope, describing its use at medical conventions around the world and inviting doctors to his Zurich clinic to watch him operate. Within just a few years, neurosurgeons everywhere had adopted the instrument as indispensable.

"It was like suddenly discovering the difference between a round wheel and a square wheel," says Lawrence Pitts, who started his brain surgery training around the time that the microscope first came into use and who later served as chief of neurosurgery at the San Francisco General Hospital. "It just changed everything." The microscope not only permitted neurosurgeons to see (and thus avoid severing) countless tiny gossamer nerves and blood vessels previously invisible to the naked eye, but the high degree of magnification also allowed them a more accurate view of the natural fissures and gaps that exist between the discrete lobes of the brain. This allowed access into deep areas of the organ either previously inaccessible to surgery, or which had necessitated cutting a path through healthy tissue, which would inevitably lead to a degree of physical or mental impairment in the patient. By the late 1960s, the intra-operative microscope was standard in neurosurgical operating rooms, and Yaşargil, who designed many of the new intracranial approaches to deep brain structures (as well as the surgical instruments to conduct those approaches), was hailed as the father of modern microneurosurgery.

Yaşargil's innovations were soon joined by a technology

Bederson consults the surgical theater scans before operating

that brought neurosurgery into the current, modern era.
In the late 1960s, Sir Godfrey Hounsfield, an electrical en-
gineer at EMI Central Research Laboratories in England,
and Allen McLeod Cormack, a South African physicist,
used multiple X-rays taken at various angles to create
pictorial "slices" of bodily organs, images that were then
reassembled with computers to create detailed 3-D repre-

sentations of that organ. The technology is called "X-ray computed tomography," or CT scan. The first CT scan on a patient's brain (using Hounsfield's and Cormack's EMI scanner) occurred on October 1, 1971, at a hospital in Wimbledon, England. It permitted unprecedentedly clear and accurate views of tumors, diseased blood vessels, and other abnormalities in the brain. If the history of neurosurgery is largely the history of improved methods for divining the location of lesions within the closed box of the obscuring skull, then the advent of CT scanning was the biggest advance in the diagnosis of brain lesions since Broca's breakthroughs in cortical localization. Hounsfield and Cormack duly shared the Nobel Prize, in 1979, for their invention.

"The CT scanner revolutionized neurosurgery more than anything else," says Phil Gutin, the chief of neurosurgery at Memorial Sloan Kettering in New York City. Gutin, who started his residency in the early 1970s, remembers the days before CT scans, when methods for trying to diagnose and locate brain lesions were not much more reliable than the techniques used by Macewen almost a hundred years earlier. Neurosurgeons had to rely on angiograms: The blood vessels of the brain were injected with a dye that could be detected by ordinary X-ray, and then the resulting dyed areas were analyzed for idiosyncrasies that might represent displaced or compressed veins and arteries. This was an attempt to divine where a lesion might lie—a highly imprecise method. "We would go to the OR and have only the vaguest idea where the tumor was," Gutin says. "There were times when we would actually miss it altogether."

In 1977, six years after the advent of the CT scanner, a still more accurate technology was invented for the detection of cancerous tumors: the magnetic resonance imaging scanner (or MRI). MRI uses large, powerful electromagnets to detect small differences in the water content of bodily tissues; because cancerous tissues have a higher water content than healthy tissues, tumors show up with great clarity in MRI scans. Like CT scanning, MRI relies on assembling multiple images to create a 3-D rendering of an organ, but because MRI is better at detecting small changes in soft tissue (like the brain), it is a more precise method for detection of tumors, and it is also safer. Unlike CT scans, which use doses of potentially harmful radiation in the form of X-rays to penetrate the body, MRI uses harmless radio waves and magnetic pulses. (MRIs are, however, considerably more expensive and take far longer.)

The greatly increased accuracy of CT and MRI scans allow neurosurgeons to plot ever narrower, less intrusive passages into the brain. Whereas a few years earlier, they might expose a full quadrant of the cortex in order to locate a tumor whose precise position could not be determined in advance, surgeons can now open tiny windows in the skull of just a few inches square, thereby reducing the risks inherent in exposing the delicate cortex. The last decade has seen further improvements in imaging with the emergence of GPS navigation and instrument tracking, as well as other computer 3-D simulations. But while such inventions have helped to reduce the risks of brain surgery, they have by no means eradicated them. All procedures ultimately come down to the skills of the surgeon: his or her manual dexterity, anatomical knowledge, and judgment during an operation. Neurosurgery still has one of the highest mortality rates of any medical specialty.

Accordingly, neurosurgeons must live with the stark reality that they will, in neurosurgeon parlance, "hurt" patients— that is, cause permanent paralysis or other dire disability, such as blindness, deafness, or persistent vegetative states, or indeed, death—even in operations that seem to have gone flawlessly. British neurosurgeon Henry Marsh, in his 2014 memoir, *Do No Harm*, was unusually candid about this side of the specialty, writing about the terrible stresses, anxieties, and stage fright that began to afflict him in his sixties, as the risks attendant on each operation, no matter how seemingly routine, weighed increasingly on him. Reading Marsh, it is impossible to escape the conclusion that it is the emotional toll of neurosurgery on its practitioners, as much as the immense technical challenges, that make it the most difficult of medical specialties—a conclusion with which Gutin agrees.

"There's just *so* much to lose," he says. "Bad results are a part of your life. I look among my colleagues here at Sloan Kettering—we have a host of surgeons here doing all manner of horrible things to different parts of the body—but as far as risk of *hurting* a patient, neurosurgery poses the greatest risk, by far. And that is very stressful. A lot of us spend time—some really bad minutes and hours—waiting for our patients to wake up from surgeries, to see if we've hurt them. And it is really, really hard."

Indeed, Gutin says, no amount of training or experience—or technology—can eliminate the danger completely, because of the maddening complexity, deep mysteries, and terrible delicacy of the brain.

"Despite a century of intense study, we still know so little about it," he says. "It's like our knowledge of the universe. We're just scratching the surface. You can believe almost nothing you hear about human intelligence and memory and the brain—our knowledge is so superficial. It is by far the most mysterious organ in the body. It's the most mysterious thing, period." He pauses, then adds, with a laugh: "To tell you the truth, we neurosurgeons don't think about that too often, or we couldn't get through a day."

4

———

The Mount Sinai neurosurgery department—comprised of offices, waiting areas, libraries, labs, and operating rooms—occupies the entire eighth floor of the Annenberg Building, a squat, featureless structure of gray stone on an unglamorous section of upper Madison Avenue, stretching from 98th to 101st Streets. Bederson's office is located down a short corridor from OR #2, his usual operating room. His office is a large suite commensurate with his status as chief of the department, a position he has held since 2007, the year he turned fifty. The front room contains his desk and computers, and a second room, through a set of sliding frosted-glass doors, holds a boardroom table where he meets with hospital brass. The area around Bederson's desk is cluttered with an array of personal mementos: photographs of his wife and two daughters, a picture of Bederson as a college gymnast doing a perfect L on the rings, and samples of his sculpture, including a small sinuous cast-bronze abstract, which sits beside a penholder on his desk, and a large

Picasso-esque head made of welded wire. Bederson's physician's assistant, Leslie Schlacter, a vivacious 6' 4" blonde who once played professional basketball for an Israeli team and now acts as Bederson's right-hand woman—scheduling his surgeries, pre-interviewing patients, even, at times, performing small operative procedures—says that she agreed to take the job only after carefully casing his office space and noting the signs of a normal domestic life and interests outside of neurosurgery. Having once worked as assistant to a doctor whose entire life was his work, Schlacter knew the danger signs. "I saw that Dr. Bederson had other outlets," she says. "Otherwise, *I'd* become his outlet."

But in some ways, the domesticating clutter around Bederson's office is deceiving, given how thoroughly, how seamlessly, he has subsumed all his interests into neurosurgery. For instance, his wife, Isabelle, is also a neurosurgeon, in his department. Their two daughters, twenty-one and eighteen, are both becoming doctors. The younger of the two, Maria, insists she will not go into neurosurgery—but she happens to be spending the summer after her freshman year in college as an unpaid intern at Mount Sinai, where, daily, she watches her father and mother operate. Her sudden decision, a few months into freshman year, to switch from a liberal arts major into pre-med was precipitated by a dramatic moment when a classmate fell ill—with a brain ailment. "I saw a friend at school have a seizure," she says. "I think a gene went off, honestly."

Bederson himself cannot pinpoint a single "Aha!" moment when he decided to become a neurosurgeon. Instead, he says, the specialty found *him*, through a series of "iterative" steps, moments of revelation and insight, which ultimately made him recognize that his various abilities and talents made him, as he puts it, a natural for the specialty. And indeed, Bederson does, in many ways, epitomize the stereotypical traits associated with neurosurgeons: He is deeply competitive, driven, intellectually brilliant. At the same time, he is honest about the doubts and misgivings that have assailed him at various points in his career. "Actually," he says, "for the longest time, I didn't think I had what it took to become a *doctor*, let alone a neurosurgeon."

Born in New York City, he was raised in the nearby suburb of Larchmont, in Westchester, the eldest of four sons of parents who were, themselves, highly distinguished in science and medicine. His father, Benjamin Bederson, is, at ninety-four, the oldest living person to have worked on the Manhattan Project, developing the atom bomb. Benjamin—the child of impoverished Russian Jewish immigrants who settled on the Lower East Side during the First World War—studied physics at City College for two years before being drafted in 1942 and assigned to a special army training program to study electrical engineering at Ohio State University. From there he was recruited, at age twenty-two, to work in the top secret Special Engineering Detachment at Los Alamos, where he helped to develop and test the triggering switches for the bombs used over Hiroshima and Nagasaki. Benjamin went on to become dean of the physics department at NYU and later the university's longtime head of the graduate school. His wife, Betty, Josh's mother, is a psychoanalyst who, in her mideighties, still works in private practice.

As a child, Bederson showed little inclination to follow his parents into medicine or science. Though clearly bright, he had what he calls "an overabundance of mental, physical, and creative energy" that made it difficult for him to concentrate in school. His psychiatrist mother, Betty, says that Bederson would, today, have earned a diagnosis of ADHD. "They almost certainly would have put that label on him," she says, "and it would have been wrong. He simply had a great deal of *energy*."

"I had this need to always get up and go and run or do something," Bederson says. One enlightened elementary-school teacher recognized this and allowed him to go outside to career around the schoolyard for five minutes every hour to calm him and help him concentrate. Gymnastics, which he started in second grade, was also a good outlet—as was another physically demanding pastime that he took up in his early teens: mountain and rock climbing, which he discovered during a summer course at NOLS, the National Outdoor Leadership School, an advanced mountaineering program created by the famous climber Peter Petzoldt. "In those days it was a thirty-day expedition," Bederson says. "You go out with a group of kids your same age with very experienced mountaineers. You learn real mountaineering, expedition planning, survival, rock climbing. I did it at age thirteen and again at fifteen."

Ultimately, however, the people he met during weekend climbing trips in the Shawgunk Mountains of upstate New York only carried him further from the academic path. "This was the early seventies and there was a whole culture of climbing and smoking pot and taking LSD and listening to the Firesign Theatre comedy troupe," Bederson says. "I got caught up in that. Grateful Dead concerts. I was too young for Woodstock, but I went to Watkins Glen. I got a little wild. Rebellious. With money I earned from an after-school job repairing windows, I secretly bought a small Honda motorcycle and kept it at a friend's house. I'd ride it around at night. What differentiated me a little bit from my friends was that at three o'clock every day I had to be ready for the gym, because I was a serious gymnast. That kind of centered me. But I was not a student."

Indeed, by the start of high school, he seemed in danger of flunking out altogether. "My father was at his wit's end," Bederson says. "We were clashing." Benjamin agrees. "I really did worry that he was on his way to become a juvenile delinquent," he says. "He was a good kid, but he was going down the wrong path." Then his mother learned about SWAS, School-within-a-School, an experimental program at Mamaroneck High for students who were bright but needed to learn creatively. "It was only for girls," Betty recalls. "But we thought it would be perfect for Josh—for the way he learned. And they took him."

"There were only nine incoming ninth-graders, and I was the only boy," Bederson says. "It was designed to do away with grades. There were only verbal descriptions of performance—a totally alternative mind-set, with small class sizes, a lot of creativity. In physics, we studied the resistance across plant leaves and did experiments to test the hypothesis that plants had feelings. It suited me well."

SWAS did not assign traditional grades for academic performance, so he held out little chance of attending a top college. His expertise as a gymnast, however, brought him to the attention of Cornell, an Ivy League university, which recruited him for their gymnastics team. "It was by far the best school I could ever hope to get into, given my lack of grades and no academic performance."

Bederson started at Cornell in the fall of 1975, became captain of the gymnastics team and, ultimately, the all-around Ivy League gymnastics champion three years in a row. His best friend, Michael Fields, a fellow freshman who is now a director of television shows and movies, remembers that Bederson, at that time, was preoccupied with trying to decide whether to try out for the Olympics. "That's the way he is: You either do things intensively and all the way or not at all," Fields says. "He used to walk along the street doing flips when he got excited. He was incredibly athletic and that is, I think, part of why, as a pure surgeon, he's so superb. He really does have amazing command of his body."

Medicine, however, was still far from Bederson's mind. "When I started at Cornell I actually told my mom that if there was one thing for sure I would never want to do is medicine, because I would not want to compete with all those pre-med students. I actually was quite afraid that I wouldn't be *able* to do it because I had no background and no track record that I could do math or science."

But among Bederson's favorite freshman classes was a course in introductory psychology taught by Ulric Neisser, the author of the 1967 book *Cognitive Psychology*, which revolutionized scientific understanding about memory and learning.

"It was a big class of 120 kids," Bederson says. "I remem-

ber the moment that made me realize I like the brain."
Neisser drew a telephone dial on the chalkboard, numbered
the finger holes from one to zero, then asked how many students thought they knew the position of the corresponding
letters on the phone dial. "All the hands went up," Bederson
says. "Because of course you know. You've seen this a thousand times, right? No one could do it! There are no letters
on the zero and the one. No one remembered that. Neisser
honed in on that observation. 'How could you not know?
You've used the phone your whole life, *looked* at that dial
countless times.' It means that the *intention* to learn is what
determines memory.

"And that fascinated me. It made me realize that the brain
is much more complicated than just a psychological thing.
There's *function* in the brain and there's also an interaction
between our intentions and the way we lay down memories.
Then we started learning about what determines forget-
ting. We learned about people with Wernicke's disorder, in
which they forget short-term memories and do things like
read the same magazine over and over again. And bit by bit
I was asking questions. And bit by bit he was directing me
to his colleagues on the neuroscience side. And the relationship rapidly developed, and within six months of arriving
in college I decided that I was going to go pre-med and become a neuroscientist of some type. But I was way behind

because I hadn't done any math or chemistry or anything. I had to enroll in summer school and do all these remedial courses."

Bederson became a living example of Neisser's theory of learning and memory. "Unless you attend to something and you *want* to do it, you don't get it," he says. "All of a sudden I wanted to do it." Bederson earned top grades in math and science courses that, a year earlier, would have stymied him. He shot to the top of his class and graduated six months early, Phi Beta Kappa, from Cornell, with a four-year bachelor of science degree. He was also accepted at one of the best medical schools in the country, UCSF, the University of California, San Francisco, School of Medicine, his top pick.

At the time, Bederson was thinking of following Neisser into neuroscience research, or even joining his mother in psychiatry—but not for long. With four months free before he was slated to start at UCSF, Bederson returned to his love for exploration and adventure—discovered at the National Outdoor Leadership School—and embarked on a solo mountaineering trip in New Zealand. On this adventure, he says, he had a series of up-close encounters with life and death that would ultimately lead him to abandon thoughts of a career in pure research, or psychiatry, and to think about specializing in some area of surgery.

The first incident occurred when he was on a ten-day

hike alone through the rain forest of Stewart Island, off the coast of New Zealand. He came upon a hunter with a wounded deer. "He had shot the deer from a helicopter, wounded him, then chased him, on foot, into the bush," Bederson says. "He was trying to kill it with a pocket knife. He couldn't get through the skin. The deer was suffering. I had a 35mm camera and I have a picture of the deer's eyes looking at me, just saying, *Do something*." Lacking any means, beyond his bare hands, for putting the deer out of its misery, Bederson decided there was only one option. "So my first medical event was to take the deer and break its neck, kill it, to end its suffering."

The next incident happened when Bederson visited nearby Fiji, staying on an island far from the coast. There, he met a missionary whose legs had swollen from elephantiasis, a potentially fatal disease of the lymph glands. "He was getting sicker and sicker and fell into septic shock. With help from his girlfriend, I got him onto a fishing boat and ferried him to a hospital on the mainland—saving his life."

The last of his epiphanies occurred a few days before he flew home to begin medical school. He was staying at a low-rent hostel in the Fijian capital of Suva. "There was a merchant marine, an Australian guy, who had just gotten married to a big Fijian woman. They got drunk and she threw him through the louvered-glass window of their room and he landed in the hall, with a deep gash in his leg. They had heard that I was a 'medical student'—which to them meant *doctor*—so they dragged him to my room. I gave him a bunch of gin, boiled a needle and thread in my cooking pot, and sewed him up and got him to the hospital. The doctors were impressed by my stitching. They didn't need to revise it. So bit by bit each one of these things led me to realize that all I really wanted to do was to *operate*. I wanted to be that person who could, with his hands, help the other person."

5

At 7:00 a.m., every Tuesday and Thursday, Bederson holds neuroradiology rounds in a large, windowless boardroom on the first floor of Mount Sinai, to discuss the brain surgeries that will be performed that day. Present are the neurosurgery residents as well as attending physicians from various specialties: pathology, radiology, oncology, anesthesiology—anyone whose expertise might have a bearing on the day's cases. The doctors sit at a long table, at one end of which are mounted several high-definition screens that beam images of the patients' CT and MRI scans. On a Thursday morning in mid-June, Bederson takes a seat at the opposite end of the table, which affords him a clear view of the screens and the assembled physicians, to whom he, as chief, directs questions.

The first case scheduled for that day is an especially dangerous and difficult one—the removal of a tumor from patient Robert O'Shea. If the frontal lobe tumor Bederson had removed, a few weeks earlier with Madani, was a finger exercise, this promises to be Rachmaninoff's Third Piano

Concerto. O'Shea, a middle-aged man, is suffering from a hemangioblastoma, a tumor that originates in the cells that line the blood vessels of the brain. His tumor had engulfed the optic chiasm—the X-shaped juncture where the two optic nerves, emerging from the back of the eyeballs, cross before entering the visual cortex. The tumor had also wrapped itself around the two internal carotid arteries that run up through the optic chiasm, which carry the brain's major blood supply from the heart. Pressure from the tumor on his optic nerves is gradually making O'Shea lose his sight. Removal of the growth would be especially difficult, since a single slip could nick the optic nerves, thus rendering him completely blind. To accidentally slice open one of the carotid arteries would cause him to bleed out on the table.

Bederson is intimately familiar with the case. He had operated on O'Shea, for this same tumor, more than a decade ago.

At that time, he had been assisting his then-boss, the former chief of neurosurgery at Mount Sinai, Dr. Kalmon Post. In a grueling six-hour operation, they had removed as much of the tumor as possible, but owing to its treacherous position, they could not remove every last cancerous cell. They were buying time until the tumor grew back. It had now grown back and was once again imperiling his vision. He was almost completely blind in his right eye and could not see well out of his left.

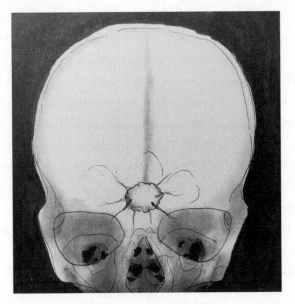

Hemangioblastoma tumor engulfing optic
nerves and carotid arteries

"Remember this case?" Dr. Post says, turning from the scan of O'Shea's brain and looking down the table at Bederson.

Post, a round-faced man of seventy-four with white hair and a small white mustache, continues to work as an attending surgeon at Mount Sinai almost ten years after stepping down as chief. He no longer does the long operations that take an especially punishing mental and physical toll, but he continues to perform a procedure for which he is an acknowledged master: transsphenoidal pituitary surgery, the procedure first pioneered by Harvey Cushing in the 1920s and later perfected by his apprentice, Norman Dott, in the 1950s, in which surgeons enter through a nostril, penetrate the bone at the back of the nose, and pass their instruments through the fissure between the two hemispheres of the brain to the pituitary. Dr. Post has performed over 3,500 of these surgeries, the second most of anyone in the country.

"Who could forget?" Bederson says in reply to Post, referring to the surgery they performed on O'Shea years before, the removal of the tumor around his optic nerves and internal carotid arteries.

"Incredible operation," Post says. "A six-hour ordeal. One of the most cardiac-inducing patients a surgeon can have."

"We were both sweating," Bederson says.

"A number of surgeons in New York deemed it inoperable," Post tells the assembled doctors. "Two *superb* people had tried it at another hospital and couldn't do it. Had to stop."

"It's amazing he's done this well," Bederson says, scrutinizing the scans, which show how fully the tumor has regrown, packing itself like a ball of Silly Putty around the optic nerves and carotids.

Schlacter, Bederson's assistant, speaks up. "He hasn't let his increasing blindness stop him from living his life. He still travels to work—alone."

"He's quite a trouper," Post says. "Amazing guy."

A screen to the right shows images from the surgical theater simulation of O'Shea's brain, a large color 3-D representation that is part of the cutting-edge imaging technology that Bederson has been acquiring in order to make Mount Sinai's neurosurgery department one of the most technologically up to date in the world. The surgical theater simulation is a virtual rendering of the brain from thousands of images taken from multiple angles, then assembled into a picture that can, with the swipe of a mouse, be rotated in any direction, up, down, or sideways. The tumor itself, color coded in blue, can, with a few clicks of the mouse, be made to turn transparent, revealing the precise anatomy of the vital structures within—thereby aiding surgeons in visualizing the arrangement of the nerves and blood vessels they are trying to avoid as they liberate them from the tumor. Bederson believes that the technology bestows on surgeons the kind of heightened 3-D spatial understanding that he innately possesses as a sculptor. "What I'm trying to do now," he says, "is use my growing interest in, and knowledge of, computers and 3-D rendering to translate, more or less, what *I* bring mentally into an operating room—to translate that into technology that assists other surgeons in visualizing the spatial anatomy."

Bederson asks his chief resident, Justin Mascitelli, to make the tumor transparent. (Chief residents are those surgeons in their seventh and final year of the neurosurgery

program; Mascitelli replaced Madani as chief resident after
Madani's departure, a week before, for Toronto and his fellowship in deep brain stimulation.) Mascitelli, who is sitting
at a computer console, clicks his mouse and the opaque blue
tumor grows pale and reveals the X shape of the optic chiasm, which is color coded yellow, and the carotid arteries,
coded red, running up through it.

"Can you turn that a bit to the left?" Bederson asks. Mascitelli sweeps the mouse and turns the entire image to the
left so that the team can see the way the tumor, which is
essentially spherical, bulges a little at the back.

"The problem is going to be controlling the bleeding
once we're into it," Bederson says. Such tumors tend to be
highly vascular—to have a great number of blood vessels
running through them. Patients can bleed to death simply
from the surgeon cutting into the tumor—yet Bederson will
have to cut into it to remove it. For this reason, he has or-
dered a large supply of extra plasma to the operating room.

The surgery is scheduled for directly after the meeting,
at 8:00 a.m. But at a few minutes to eight, Bederson's smartphone vibrates. A resident informs him that O'Shea is refus-
ing to undergo the operation. This is a calamity on many
levels, including financial. The dollar cost of preparing a patient for surgery at a hospital like Mount Sinai runs into the
tens of thousands of dollars for blood workups, angiograms,

brain scans, and other pre-operative procedures. The eleventh-hour cancellation also wreaks havoc on the department logistics, where scheduling of the four operating rooms is as finely worked out as the take-offs and landings at JFK airport.

Bederson puts away his smartphone. "He says he doesn't want the operation," he tells the room. "He's scared."

"Let's go up and talk to him," says Post.

Bederson gestures at Rui, the third-year medical student, to join them, as well as Mascitelli. It's not every day that a patient, minutes before going into major surgery, backs out. Bederson figures this might be a teachable moment. Dr. Post joins them. As they enter the elevator to take them up to the eighth floor, Post tells Bederson that he will not be at the hospital the following week. He is taking three weeks off for the summer. Bederson gapes at him, stunned. "You've never done that before!" Bederson says.

"Not since 1985," Post says. "Never wanted to miss what was going on here. Never wanted to be gone that long."

Bederson turns to Rui and Mascitelli. "That's because it's not work," he says. "It isn't work for us."

"That's absolutely true," Post says.

At the eighth floor, the elevator doors open and the group exits onto the neurosurgery ward. They make their way down a series of corridors, past the Malis Library and Bederson's office, until they come to a pair of large swinging doors that lead into the neurosurgery holding area where patients wait before going into the OR. It's a bustling space full of nurses, anesthesiologists, surgeons, residents, visiting family members, and up to three patients at a time, who lie on rolling beds, separated one from another by hanging curtains. Someone has thought to push O'Shea's bed into a small adjoining room so that the doctors can have some privacy as they talk to him.

Bederson and his entourage enter the room. O'Shea is sitting up in his hospital bed. Except for a slightly wandering right eye, it would be hard to detect that he is suffering significant blindness. The team takes up positions around the bed, taking care not to crowd him.

O'Shea is well aware of the risks the operation poses and expresses fears that something unexpected will take place during the surgery.

Post takes the lead. "The OR is the most monitored place in the hospital," he says in a quiet, kindly voice, "a place where we can react to any emergency. So there's nothing to worry about. We've assembled the team, and it's a big team."

"I was reading about my tumor," O'Shea says, "and you can't take all of it out anyway." (He is referring to how neurosurgeons, owing to the treacherous location of this particular kind of tumor, cannot remove every cancerous cell, for fear of damaging the optic nerves.)

"That's true," Post says. "But we can get a *lot* of it, and this will stop it from pressing on your optic nerve and this will be an improvement. No medicine can shrink it, and radiation is too dangerous. I can't drag you kicking and screaming, but this really is the right thing to do. The only thing."

Post steps away from the bed and mumbles, "Feels strange to be twisting his arm. My wife is a bio-ethicist. Pushing patients is not something you want to do."

Bederson has been standing silently at the end of the bed, his hand resting gently on O'Shea's foot, touching it lightly through the bedclothes, a gesture he often makes with patients, to establish a human connection, to reassure them. He now leans over the bed, listening to O'Shea, who is saying to him, "You're the one who is going to be doing the surgery anyway, right?" Bederson tells him that this is correct. "Well," he says, "I need to think about it."

"That's fine," Bederson says. "I'll come back and talk to you then." But he has already taken a psychological read of the situation—and made a decision. "He won't do it," Bederson says, definitively, once he and the team are out in the hall. "At least not today."

Accordingly, he schedules another procedure for OR #2—an operation on a patient who has suffered a ruptured brain aneurysm. Aneurysms are defects in blood vessels, small outpouchings on the side of an artery where the wall of the vessel is thin and blood builds up as in a small balloon. And as when a balloon is overfilled with liquid, such lesions can, under pressure of blood pumped from the heart, burst, causing a subarachnoid hemorrhage—uncontrolled bleeding into the space between the "arachnoid" membrane that encases the brain and the brain itself. Burst aneurysms often result in what sufferers describe as "the worst headache of my life" (a complaint so common that neurosurgeons have reduced it to the acronym WHOML, as in, "The patient came to Emergency complaining of WHOML"). If not treated in a timely fashion—usually by the swift removal of part of the skull to allow the swollen brain to expand—the syndrome frequently results in permanent brain damage or death.

The patient Bederson now prepares to operate on was admitted to the hospital a week ago with a severe subarachnoid hemorrhage. A section of skull had been removed to allow the patient's brain to expand, the bleeding had been halted and the patient had stabilized. But now fresh complications had developed: namely, a dangerous buildup of cerebrospinal fluid or CSF—the clear, colorless, shock-absorbing liquid in which the brain and spinal column are bathed. An excess of the liquid (which is generated by three balloon-like cavities at the center of the brain) can be fatal, crowding out healthy brain tissue, crushing and killing it.

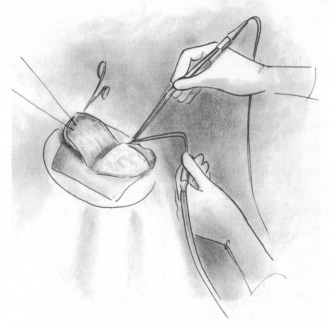

Cauterizing the edge of the scalp flap before opening the skull

To tap the excess CSF, surgeons place what is called a ventriculo peritoneal or VP shunt, a long flexible tube that collects the fluid from the brain ventricles (hence, "ventriculo") and diverts it to the abdominal cavity, or peritoneum (hence, "peritoneal") where it can be safely absorbed by the body. With today's patient, Bederson removes the bone flap that had earlier been cut in the skull to alleviate pressure on the brain, then inserts one end of the tubing into the ventricle where it will collect the cerebrospinal fluid. He then cuts a small incision at the base of the neck and uses a long rigid hollow metal rod to irrigate a canal, under the skin, running from the neck down to the lower abdomen. There, he cuts another small incision, through which he pushes the end of the irrigation rod. He then feeds the flexible rubber tubing into the rod, guides it down to the abdomen, then pulls it out through the end of the hollow rod. He extracts the rod, leaving the tube in place, then sews its lower end into the abdominal cavity. As he works, Bederson explains to Rui, who is observing the operation, that the placing of a VP shunt requires hundreds of minutely rehearsed moves, all of which must be performed in the correct order. "It's the simplest of neurosurgical procedures," he says. "But it's all about the littlest details that make or break a case."

He's an hour into the procedure when a resident sticks his head into the OR and says that O'Shea has had a sudden change of heart. He is now willing to undergo the surgery on the tumor wrapped around his optic nerves and carotid arteries. Bederson glances at his watch. It's almost noon. Too late, in his view, to start so complex a procedure.

"No," he says. "What is it today—Friday? We'll try on Monday."

6

After his trip to New Zealand, Bederson started medical school at UCSF in the fall of 1979. The first two years of the four-year MD degree are devoted to classroom lectures in subjects foundational to all medical specialties, including anatomy, biochemistry, pharmacology, microbiology, immunology, infectious diseases, and pathology. Bederson earned honors in all his subjects and meanwhile explored his options for what specialty to go into. Despite his epiphany in the down-at-heels Fijian hostel about a career in some area of surgery, he was, in his first year of medical school, keeping his mind open to all possibilities.

"I was meeting the psychiatrists, the neurologists, the transplant surgeons, the hand surgeons, OBGYN." He indulged a brief flirtation with international health and used his credentials as class president of the American Medical Student Association to secure a four-week trip to Malaysia as part of an infectious diseases rotation—partly an excuse for another exotic adventure. "I went all over Malaysia, saw the Straits of Malacca, the spine of mountains in the middle where the Thai insurgents were coming down, went to remote rural clinics, got to deliver babies—just amazing. I wrote a paper and presented it at the AMA student association, but then I kind of ruled out international medicine. I realized I wasn't interested in it. So doing these things, lobbing out these questions and having these adventures, each time I would bounce back to the brain."

His earlier interest in the brain had been from a research perspective. Now he was daring to think about brain *surgery* but doubted he had what it took. "I still did not have the faith in myself that I could go to this *highest* level," he says.

But then he spoke with Phil Gutin, who was at that time a senior neurosurgery resident at UCSF's famed Brain Tumor Research Center. Medicine is an apprenticeship profession, one in which mentoring is crucial to the passing down of knowledge and the shaping of careers, and Gutin, sensing Bederson's burgeoning interest in neurosurgery, brought him into the OR to witness a procedure, a craniotomy to remove a tumor. Bederson was transfixed. Emboldened, he asked Gutin about the steps he would have to take in order to become a neurosurgeon. Gutin, a product of UCSF's trainee program, which places a premium on the importance of research, urged Bederson to find a position in a neuroscience lab. Gutin, who is now the chairman of the neurosurgery department at New York's Memorial Sloan Kettering Cancer Center, one of the top programs in the country, still counsels young neurosurgical hopefuls to take a research path. "You have to differentiate yourself from the masses of medical students who want to get into a good neurosurgery program," Gutin says. "You have to prove yourself. Be it neuroscience investigation or brain tumor investigation—something that shows that you're serious about wanting to advance the specialty."

Gutin introduced Bederson to two neurosurgeons, Lawrence Pitts and Henry Bartkowski, who ran a neurological research laboratory at San Francisco General Hospital. Pitts and Bartkowski were studying brain injury from trauma and strokes, and they wanted to develop animal experiments to look at how various treatments might help reduce the resulting paralysis. "We wanted to create a model that replicates the human disease and is itself reproducible," says Pitts. They assigned Bederson the task of designing experiments using laboratory rats. Over the course of his second year at medical school, Bederson devised methods for inducing variable-sized strokes in rats by blocking their middle cerebral artery, the main blood vessel that carries blood from the heart into the brain; he then measured the precise degree of paralysis in their limbs, correlating the limb deficit to the size of the infarction—the term used to describe the area of dead, blood-starved tissue in the brain. Then, using a control group of his paralyzed subjects, he conducted experiments to see whether a particular drug, a calcium channel blocker, when administered after the onset of a stroke, reduced the paralysis. "Josh, even back then, was a very fine technical surgeon," says Pitts, "and he developed the model—a little filament blockage of an artery that could then be removed to restore blood flow. It was very tricky to expose a tiny artery in a rat brain, to open it, so that you could put the small filament in, then to take the filament out and repair the artery and have that be repeated over a number of animals, so that you had a population that all behaved roughly the same way—he did a really terrific technical job."

Bederson's research also provided valuable clinical information that the surgeons were able to apply to their human patients. "One of the questions that Josh's model specifically looked at was: What if you turn off the flow to the brain in one artery for a period of time, then reopen the flow to the brain in that same artery?" Pitts says. "Now, the clinical situation, in humans, would be if a small blood clot went to a brain artery and you then had a way to remove it—which you can do with small catheters and take the clot out. But is that a good thing or a bad thing to do? Turns out if you take the clot out quickly and restore the blood flow, then you certainly can recover some of the injured brain to the point of reversing the injury. In other instances, if you take the clot out after too long a period of time, it makes the stroke *worse*. You get hemorrhage into the stroke. Josh's research was helpful in exposing that."

Despite Bederson's successes in the lab and his excellent grades, which put him on track to get into one of the best neurosurgery programs, he retained a strong element of the restlessness that propelled him, as a child, to want to get up and run around and explore new things. Which, he says, helps to explain his next, highly unusual move.

He had continued, in his spare time, to sculpt. Midway through his second year of medical school, he took photographs of several of his completed sculptures "on a whim" and sent them to various graduate school art departments. He was invited to join NYU's master of fine arts program. He knew how high the stakes were.

"Neurosurgery is the most competitive specialty," he says. "If you deviate—if you do anything crazy and you're not at the top—you won't get in." Nevertheless, NYU's offer was too exciting to pass up. He insists that this detour reflected not a wavering in his resolve to pursue neurosurgery but, paradoxically, its opposite. "I'd gone all the way through high school and college not knowing what I was going to do as a career—finally I knew what I was going to do: I was going to be a neurosurgeon. With that in mind, I knew that I could now take time off!"

His adviser at the time was Nick Feduska, the chairman of the transplantation program at UCSF. Feduska warned him that an appearance of inconstancy or lack of focus could hurt his chances of getting into a neurosurgery program. Bederson assured him that, despite his proposed detour from medicine, he was wholly committed to neurosurgery and vowed, during his art school year, to write up for publication the rat research he had done in Pitts and Bartkowski's lab. Feduska, with some reservations, gave Bederson his blessing.

Bederson moved to New York, where he rented a fifth-floor walk-up on the corner of Jane Street and West 4th in Greenwich Village. By day, he took classes in drawing, painting, sculpture, and art history, and he worked on a series of progressively larger sculptural works in various mediums: marble, steel, cast iron, wire. By night, he retired to the Loeb Library to write up his rat stroke research. To support himself, he took a part-time job as a phlebotomist, drawing blood, at St. Vincent's Catholic Medical Center on 12th Street—and found himself, by chance, at the epicenter of what would emerge as the biggest medical crisis of the era. "There were all these men coming in with purple splotches, emaciated, for blood tests," Bederson recalls. "It was 1983, the height of the AIDS epidemic—but before we even had a name for it. We had no idea what we were dealing with."

Bederson's year in New York culminated with his landing a one-man show at an art gallery on West 4th Street, a considerable achievement. But if his art school detour was, however subconsciously, a testing of the waters for a career change, the result was much like his earlier adventure in international health in Malaysia.

He bounced back to the brain.

7

On Monday morning, Robert O'Shea, the hemangio-blastoma patient, is still agreeing to the surgery.

A few minutes before eight, when the operation is scheduled to begin, Bederson visits him in the holding area. O'Shea is asking a series of questions. He wants to know about the steroids that will be prescribed after the surgery to prevent brain swelling; about the recovery time; about the size of the incision and its visibility. Bederson answers each question patiently. "The incision will be completely invisible," he says. "It's a long incision that goes across the back of the head. We hide it inside your hair. We actually learned this from plastic surgeons."

Dr. Post arrives to lend O'Shea moral support. The patient greets him with a smile. "You're in better spirits today," Post says. "That's good. I expect those eyes to be a bit better. Let's hope so."

An orderly appears, grasps the back of O'Shea's rolling bed, and wheels him through the doors that lead to OR #2.

Ordinarily, Bederson would leave the patient preparation to his chief resident, Mascitelli, but the unusual cir-
cumstances surrounding today's operation compel him to a
more hands-on approach. After O'Shea has been put under,
Bederson helps prep his hair for the incision, using a comb
to make a part that runs across the back of the head. He is in
a quiet, self-contained mood, as if about to face a dangerous
and decisive battle.

When he is finished with O'Shea's hair, Bederson consults
a large computer screen mounted to the left of the patient:
the surgical theater 3-D simulation with its color-coded
representation of the tumor wrapped around O'Shea's optic
chiasm and internal carotid arteries. Bederson sweeps his
finger over the screen, causing the head to rotate so that
he can see the back of the tumor. "This is stable," he tells
Mascitelli, "because it was radiated." He looks closely at the
screen and notes how the tumor has engulfed the right optic
nerve. "His left eye is better than his right," he says.

Bederson's daughter Maria will be observing this operation, and he now explains to her how he will "debulk"
the tumor, then gently lift the remaining growth off the
delicate nerves and arteries. "I'll be avoiding these 'no fly'
zones," he says, pointing at the surgical theater simulation
where four small round balls, at critical spots on the optic

nerves and carotids, indicate where it would be disastrous to stray. "We're going to enter through the Sylvian fissure to minimize tissue manipulation and potential damage to the brain."

The brain is divided symmetrically through its midline into the left and right hemispheres, each of which is in turn divided into five separate pieces, or lobes—the left and right frontal lobes, at the front of the brain, behind the forehead; the parietal lobes, across the top of the head; the occipital lobes, at the back of the head; and the temporal lobes, at the temples, just in front of the ears. The narrow gaps, or fissures, between the various lobes permit neurosurgeons to enter into deeper areas of the brain. The horizontal gap that separates the parietal lobes on top of the brain from the temporal lobes below is called the Sylvian fissure, and it is one of the so-called "intracranial" approaches made possible by the advent of the intra-operative microscope and pioneered by Yaşargil decades ago.

"Should be quite a case," Bederson says.

By 11:20 a.m., Mascitelli has O'Shea's head open. Bederson settles into the operating chair. He looks at the hole that Mascitelli has drilled in the skull and is not happy with the top edge of the opening: It does not give him enough freedom of movement to get his instruments in and around the tricky tumor. Bederson asks for the drill and swiftly buzzes away another two centimeters from the top of the window. He then asks the scrub nurse for the instruments: forceps and sucker. With the forceps he probes and picks at the tissues lightly, using what he calls "haptic feedback"— the actual *feel* of the tissue's consistency through his instruments, which long experience has taught him to pick up through the nerve endings in his fingertips. This feedback aids him in planning his attack on the tumor, each exploratory touch telling him something about the growth's density, size, consistency. Tumors can vary in texture from hard pebble-like growths that cling stubbornly to healthy brain, to areas that are as soft as oatmeal and can be sucked relatively easily from normal tissue, and everything in between. As he works, Bederson notes that the brain, slightly swollen, is bulging out of the skull cavity.

"We want to drain some CSF and relax the brain," he says. An assistant taps the spinal drain, draining off the excess cerebrospinal fluid. The brain immediately shrinks back into the skull like a deflating balloon. Now Bederson can set his retractors. He places the blades of the broad L-shaped instrument into the Sylvian fissure and gently eases the lobes apart. Now he can see, through the microscope's stereo eyepieces, part of the optic nerve, which, under high magnification, looks like a thick cable. Ordi-

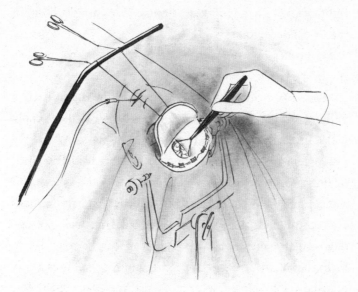

A "keyhole" skull opening for removing a tumor

narily, a healthy optic nerve looks white as bone. Half of O'Shea's nerve is shrouded in a red substance. "Tumor is right on it," he says.

For several minutes he explores, very gently moving healthy brain tissue out of the way with retractors and pulling away at the tumor until a movement of his forceps uncovers another glint of whiteness amid the blood and tissue.

"Now," he says, "there's the opposite optic nerve—right where it's supposed to be." This nerve, running from the right eye, is fully engulfed in tumor. "He's almost blind in that eye," Bederson says.

He pushes lightly on the section of tumor that lies between the two optic nerves.

"Feels like foam rubber—bouncy. See, the tumor itself is pulsating. That gives you some idea of the vascular supply within it. Let's cut into it. Usually it's not pleasant."

He gently slices the tumor with a short-bladed scalpel, opening a tiny incision in its surface. Blood gushes from the cut and wells up in the wound. Bederson calmly sucks away the blood, then stanches the bleeding with cotton-oids—small pieces of absorbent cotton—and a coagulating foam that he dispenses into the wound. He then uses a pair of cauterizing bipolar tweezers to seal the edges of the cut, administering short bursts of heat through the tips of the tweezers by stepping on a pedal under his left foot. The cauterizing tool makes a loud snapping sound, like corn kernels popping. Gently, carefully, he sucks away at the soft inner part of the tumor that he has exposed with his small incision, debulking it.

Dr. Post, who feels a certain emotional investment in this case—given his earlier role as lead surgeon more than a decade ago and the drama over the canceled operation last week—arrives in the operating room to watch Bederson work. The view through Bederson's eyepieces is projected on several 2-D screens mounted around the room, including on the base of the intra-operative microscope. Post watches this screen as Bederson places the end of an ultrasound wand against the exposed right carotid artery, one of two major blood vessels that carry blood from the heart, nourishing the brain. The room fills with the rhythmic whooshing sound of the patient's blood thrumming through the artery.

"Doesn't *sound* like a nerve," Post jokes.

"Yes," Bederson says. "Let's stay out of that."

Post is unable to resist a pedagogic observation for his former underling. "That carotid is closer than you think," he tells Bederson. "It's good you've got it mapped out. That 3-D view in your mind is going to be precious."

"Ever seen this type of tumor before?" asks Mascitelli, who is standing beside Bederson and watching through the second set of eyepieces on the microscope.

"Yeah," Bederson says, "but I'm not sure I've ever taken one from between the optic nerves before. Kal did it last time."

He works for ten minutes, silently, gingerly sucking tumor off the right optic nerve, then carefully cutting open a slit in the membrane that sheathes the nerve, in order to reduce the pressure of cerebrospinal fluid that has built up beneath the membrane—a process known as decompressing the nerve. "I've gotten the right optic reasonably well decompressed," he says, at length. "If I try to reach around the left optic, I might damage it, so let's shift position." They reset the retractors and lights to come at the tumor from a new angle. "We're doing an interhemispherical approach now," Bederson says, referring to the fact that he has shifted from using the Sylvian fissure as a route toward the tumor and is now going in through the vertical, midline gap that divides the brain into left and right hemispheres.

To the untrained eye, it all looks hopelessly undefined, undifferentiated. Pools of blood, soft brain tissue, glinting nerves, and thick blood vessels.

Dr. Lee's voice comes from the foot of the bed, a slight tilt of urgency in his tone. "Blood pressure just dropped," he says.

Bederson's reply is calm: "I was putting pressure on his left carotid. I've taken it off now."

Lee reports that O'Shea's blood pressure is returning to normal.

Bederson continues to crawl deeper toward the center of O'Shea's brain, advancing slowly with his instruments, gently pushing aside healthy tissue with the cottonoids as shock absorber. "There is the pituitary gland . . ." he murmurs. "Everything we've done up to now was preparation for this view," Bederson says. It's two o'clock, and he has been operating for six hours. "We couldn't have seen this before."

He operates, delicately lifting the diseased tissue away from the surface of the brain, to which the tumor is attached by innumerable tiny blood vessels that nourish the cancerous growth. He cuts and cauterizes the blood vessels—a process known in neurosurgery as "developing the plane." His body remains relaxed, his hand motions graceful, fluid, but a palpable sense of tension has come into the room as he gets closer and closer to the left optic nerve, a holding-the-breath atmosphere, the only sound the steady *beep beep beep* of the blood pressure monitor. He's operating right on the chiasm, within a fraction of a millimeter of the blue spheres that, on the surgical theater simulation, demarcate the no-fly zone. Because his body seems so relaxed, his shoulders hanging loose, his arms propped casually on the armrests, it comes as a shock when he suddenly lets out a long, loud groan: "*Eeeaugh!*" After a moment, he speaks.

"So hard to get it off. I can't be too aggressive or he'll be completely blind."

He operates for a while in silence.

"I'm gonna see if I can come back around and get between the optic nerve and the carotid. I think we're decompressing it pretty well from the medial side. It's a minute-to-minute trade-off between tumor removal and how gentle we have to be with his eyes."

He operates for another few minutes in silence.

"Ahhhh," he again groans. "It's not well decompressed."

He changes his angle of attack. With his left foot pedal he increases the magnification of the right optic nerve. The white bone-like structure looks as if it is coated in a thick, sticky substance, like spaghetti sauce, red and slightly lumpy. The question in neurosurgery is always: When to leave well enough alone? The balance between caution and aggression—the dichotomy Bederson laid out for Madani two weeks ago, during removal of the frontal lobe tumor, when he spoke about trying to find the balance between ability and confidence. Bederson wavers. Suddenly he wants his former boss's opinion. "Once someone is your chief, they're always your chief," he will say later. "And I feel that way about Dr. Post." But Post has left the OR.

"Will someone go and ask Kal if he could take a look at this?" Bederson says.

Post comes back into the room and looks at the screen. Innately more cautious than Bederson, Post would not dream of flying a private aircraft as Bederson has, to say nothing of mountain climbing and hang gliding—and he rejects the widely held notion that all neurosurgeons are risk-taking types. "I think it's more that we're used to *accepting* risk," he says. "I don't know that it's a desire to do extreme sports and things like that." Peering now at the stubborn tumor clinging to O'Shea's optic nerve, Post says, on a note of warning, "If there isn't a really good plane where you can peel that off the nerve, you might have to leave it. He'll be irradiated there anyway." He leans closer to the screen. "I'm seeing a carpet of tumor over the whole nerve. If it's not coming off . . ."

The words seem to act on Bederson like a challenge, giving him courage. He asks for a pair of scissors. With the points of the scissors, working with heart-stopping closeness to the no-fly zone, he snips at the interface between the tumor and the nerve. "Maybe . . . I can . . . separate it . . ." Bederson says. He manages to free up a corner of the tumor. He asks for a pair of forceps. He lightly grasps the micromillimeter-wide edge of the tumor that he has freed up and peels it away from the nerve, exposing fresh white surface.

"There!" Post cries. "Looks like you're accomplishing something!"

"Yup," Bederson says. "I'm getting more of it now. Much better, right?"

He pauses to look at his handiwork. He says that he thinks this is as far as he can safely go. Everyone else in the room tacitly agrees. It's almost four o'clock. The operation is over.

Bederson stands and strips off his gloves. "Certainly decompressed the nerve," he tells his daughter Maria, who looks on with awe and disbelief. "I did *not* think we were going to get that last part. Now, whether his optic nerve tolerates everything we did, we will find out. Certainly hope so. The optic is not very forgiving."

8

The final two years of medical school liberate students from the classroom. They go on to hospital wards and deal with actual patients in a series of three-month rotations in specialties that include internal medicine, general surgery, pediatrics, obstetrics and gynecology, and urology. Third year is when most medical students decide what specialty they want to go into, and they devote themselves, single-mindedly, to pursuing that goal.

When Bederson resumed his medical degree in third year, after his foray into art school at NYU, he at first tried to keep up his extracurricular interests, renting a 3,000-square-foot art studio space in the abandoned Triple A shipyards on the Oakland Bay and taking a course in hang gliding off the cliffs of San Francisco Bay. "I made it to USGS Level 2, advanced beginner," he says, "but I quit after a near fatal accident—the result of fatigue." It was a harsh wake-up call. He was forced to acknowledge that, if he wanted to qualify for one of the top neurosurgery programs, he was going to have to give medical school all his energy, mental and physical. He signed over the lease on his art studio to a friend, abandoned hang gliding, and ceased his weekend forays to Yosemite to rock climb. His first clinical rotation was in internal medicine. "You get graded with pass, fail, or honors—and earning honors was a really important goal," he says. "I wanted to prove myself. I read everything. I was *so* up to date. I was able to quote every possible study. I just immersed myself."

At the same time, his rat research papers began appearing in respected medical journals, including *Stroke*. The first of these, "Rat middle cerebral artery occlusion: evaluation of the model and development of a neurologic examination," is, thirty years later, cited frequently by other scientists. The system Bederson created for measuring the degree of paralysis in the limbs of laboratory rats, the Bederson Score for Rat Neurological Deficits, is now standard in laboratories. "Those papers totally set me apart from the other med students," he says. "And they allowed me to re-establish my seriousness, even though I did this thing—an art school MFA—that did not compute. I was gunning for neurosurgery."

At that time, the top two neurosurgery programs in the country were Columbia University Medical Center, in New York, and the neurosurgery department at Bederson's own medical school, UCSF. Most gave the edge to UCSF, in large part because of the reputation of the chief of the neurosurgery department, Dr. Charles Byron Wilson, who, although then only in his fifties, was already a legendary figure in the specialty. Wilson was the subject of a 1999 article in the *New Yorker*, by Malcolm Gladwell, about the mysteries of "physical genius," where his preternatural talents as a surgeon were likened to Wayne Gretzky's gifts as a hockey player and Yo-Yo Ma's as a musician. Performing complicated and dangerous brain surgeries with an unmatched speed and precision (an operation that might take any other neurosurgeon several hours to do, Wilson could perform in twenty-five minutes), he routinely performed up to eight surgeries a day, while at the same time heading up the country's first research laboratory exclusively devoted to brain tumors, training residents (a startling number of whom, like Bederson and Gutin, went on to become chief at top neurosurgical programs), and running eighty miles a week.

Wilson was particularly adept at the so-called "bomb disposal" operation of brain surgery: the placement of tiny titanium clips across the narrow neck of aneurysms, the small, balloon-like outpouchings that develop on the sides of arteries where the vessel wall is thin and that can fatally rupture. A congenital defect that runs in families, aneurysms are often detected, by brain scan, only after another family member has died from one that has burst. Their surgical "defusing" is especially dangerous since the aneurysm must first be delicately separated from the surrounding brain tissue to which it is attached—a procedure known as "dissecting" the aneurysm—before being clipped. Such manipulations are intensely dangerous since aneurysms, full to bursting with pressurized blood, can explode at a gentle touch. Wilson made the procedure "look easy," Gladwell wrote, and he quoted one of Wilson's former residents: "'After he'd dissected the whole aneurysm out, and when he had control of all the feeding vessels, I'd see him grasp it and flip it back and forth, because he somehow *knew* that if it popped he would still be able to clip it . . . Most people are afraid of aneurysms. He wasn't afraid of them at all. He was like a cat playing with a mouse.'"

Bederson first came to Wilson's attention while doing his third-year medical school rotation in neurosurgery. Wilson was an intimidating presence, demanding and prickly, but Bederson quickly established a rapport with him. "We saw a patient who was very dark skinned but with Caucasian features," Bederson recalls. "She was walking down the hall far away, and I said, 'Dr. Wilson, does she have Nelson's syndrome?' It's when you have very high cortisol levels and your adrenals have been removed so your skin turns very dark. I'd read about it in passing and it happened to be something that he was interested in. My curiosity and my ability to call back certain things I'd read and my ability to communicate with him in a way that was natural made me rise in his eyes. I came to his attention."

He stayed on Wilson's radar. As part of his neurosurgery rotation, Bederson began to accompany one of Wilson's senior residents on daily rounds. Because of Wilson's phenomenal productivity, there were always scores of patients whose post-operative condition needed to be closely monitored for signs of complications. Wilson, who took every Wednesday off, expected to be kept up to date, in minute detail, on the condition of all his patients.

"He would call at 8:30 a.m., sharp, on Wednesdays," Bederson says. "His resident would have to round on all his patients—frequently fifteen or twenty patients—and have *all* the results by the time Dr. Wilson called. Being Wilson's chief resident was the hardest thing in the world, and when I was a medical student, there was a resident who was not up to the task. He wouldn't be ready when Wilson called." Bederson began to cover for him. "So I was standing there, by his side, every time he would take that phone call, and bit by bit, Charlie started asking to speak to me."

In his final year of med school, Bederson applied to several top neurosurgical programs. Like today, the top schools had an acceptance rate of under 1 percent of applicants. Bederson was accepted at his two top picks, which happened to be the acknowledged best programs in the country: UCSF and Columbia in New York. "Ultimately, I gave the edge to UCSF," he says, "because of Wilson."

All neurosurgical residencies are demanding. Residency under Wilson was, by all accounts, brutal. Driving his trainees as hard as he drove himself, Wilson held medical rounds at six o'clock every morning and mercilessly grilled residents on the latest medical literature. In the OR, he was unforgiving. "It was constant criticism," says Sloan Kettering chief Phil Gutin. "He wasn't a friend of the residents. It's almost like it was a studied thing, the remoteness. But it drove us." Gladwell cited a former Wilson resident who developed a chronic eyelid twitch that didn't stop until he moved on to train with someone else.

Bederson, however, thrived. "Josh was a particularly talented surgeon," says Gutin. "The most important thing that differentiates residents is their ability to push the case from Point A to Point B, and not floundering and getting lost in the middle, or not knowing what the next step is—it's having an engine to drive you through a case with some eye to getting the damn thing done. Josh had that."

"If your God-given talents matched what Dr. Wilson wanted, and what he demanded, you did well," says Bederson. "And then you were given opportunities that no one else could ever have. If you did not . . ."

Bederson says that his co-resident, a Harvard graduate brilliant enough to have written and published a novel while still a medical student, struggled under Wilson. "He was obviously a talented, intelligent human being. But his communication style, his physicality, his speed, his efficiencies, his *whatever*, did not match what Dr. Wilson needed, and he came very close to being fired. He was given a remedial year, and he suffered." Many were not given the chance for a remedial year. In the seven years that Bederson spent as a neurosurgery trainee at UCSF, Wilson fired 50 percent of the residents. "Charlie was ruthless," Bederson says. "Of the twenty-two that should have graduated in that time, eleven lost their jobs. It was the most devastating event of their lives."

Wilson is now eighty-seven years old and lives in an assisted-care facility. But he was willing to answer questions, submitted via email, about his training of residents. He is unapologetic about his draconian treatment of his trainees. "I was honest about firing," he writes. "I told them they were too smart to be a poor neurosurgeon and I didn't think they had the aptitude to do it, and that they could be very good at something else. It's the department chair's responsibility to see that someone who will not be able to serve patients well does not just get passed down or up the line—because of the potential danger to patients in a very dangerous field." Wilson says that Bederson came to his attention early and quickly distinguished himself as an exceptional trainee. "I observed his movements in the hospital and the operating room, and I saw that he carried himself with composure—he never seemed rushed and he always got an amazing amount done. I had no doubt that he would rise to the top of his profession—and he has."

Wilson encouraged all his residents to augment their experience in the OR with intensive laboratory research, as Wilson himself did. Bederson had already made a name for himself with his rat stroke papers and could have continued his research in the area of vascular neurosurgery—that part of the specialty that deals with blood flow to the brain. Instead, he sought out a position in a research lab run by Howard Fields, a renowned neuroscientist who was a founder of the UCSF pain management center. It was, Bederson says, a rare wrong turn.

"I was doing single-unit recordings of the rostral ventral medial medulla, because I thought I was going to be interested in deep brain stimulation for pain management and consciousness. At that time, we thought that we could reverse coma and control pain by stimulating very specific areas of the brain—the so-called Gate Control theory, which was generating a lot of interest."

But an explosion of advances in pain management through drug therapies and other means, in the late 1980s, soon rendered deep brain stimulation techniques redundant, and Bederson now regrets the time he lost in Fields's lab. "I should have just stayed on my focus on vascular neurosurgery, and I would have been far more productive," he says. "I regret that. I only have about one hundred papers published." (Wilson, by comparison, has published over six hundred.) "I think my academic career suffered as a result of that lack of continuity. It was an error in judgment. I thought I was really going to go in this area. What I discovered was that I hated those patients, I did not like dealing with them, and I thought the surgery was incredibly boring. Someone should have told me, 'Josh, you're not cut out for this.' That was a wrong turn. I corrected, though."

9

Despite the heavy manipulation of his optic nerves during the removal of the hemangioblastoma that had engulfed his optic chiasm and internal carotid arteries, Robert O'Shea tolerates the operation well. After a week of recovery in the hospital, he is released and eventually returns to work. The vision in his right eye does not, however, return, as hoped—nor does it even improve. But it is no longer deteriorating, and in neurosurgery such small blessings must often be counted as major successes. Death or dire disability are always possible outcomes, and every person who sets out to become a neurosurgeon must be prepared to form a particularly intimate relationship with mortality. This is acutely apparent a few days after O'Shea's surgery, when Bederson treats a patient named Henry Rodriguez.

Four months earlier, Rodriguez, a shy, soft-spoken man in his late twenties, came to Mount Sinai complaining of a sudden, unexplained paralysis down his right side. He also had some trouble forming words. Up until then, he had been perfectly healthy, a worker who did rigorous manual labor. A brain scan showed an irregular patch of bright white among the gray mass of healthy tissue—a frightening sight. Blood shows up as white on the black-and-white scans. It was clear that Rodriguez was suffering from bleeding in his brain, but there were no obvious signs of a tumor or a ruptured aneurysm. He was kept under observation, and when it was noted that the bleeding in his brain had stopped, and his blood pressure had returned to normal, he was sent home. But he was soon back. "He looked sleepy, out of it," Bederson says. "And he was ataxic"—he had trouble keeping his balance. A new brain scan revealed signs of hydrocephalus, a buildup of cerebrospinal fluid in the brain. He was admitted for emergency surgery and Bederson placed a VP shunt to drain the excess CSF. Ordinarily, a patient would rapidly improve. Rodriguez got worse, his balance deteriorating, his speech becoming more slurred. In mid-June, he returned to the hospital and was given an MRI. In the intervening weeks, his body had absorbed the blood that had invaded his brain tissues, so the cloud of white had disappeared from the scan. With the blood gone, Bederson could now see a previously hidden tumor on the left side of his brain. The tumor was in an area of the cortex that neurosurgeons call the "eloquent brain," that which is implicated in speech, certain motor movements, and other higher brain functions. Furthermore, the tumor was not of the spherical, self-contained type that suggests a growth on the benign end of the spectrum. Quite the contrary. This tumor was of an irregular shape, with tentacles extending into the surrounding brain tissue, suggestive of an aggressively spreading malignancy.

Bederson and his assistant, Schlacter, met with Rodriguez in Bederson's office to give him the bad news. They explained that Rodriguez could not go home, as he had hoped, but instead would have to go into emergency surgery, first thing in the morning, so that Bederson could remove the tumor and biopsy it, to determine what kind of cancer it was. All indications from the scan suggested a glioblastoma multiforme, the most aggressive form of brain cancer, for which life expectancy is less than a year. Bederson kept this dire possibility to himself for the time being, but he was obliged to inform Rodriguez that he was in all likelihood harboring a malignant brain tumor. Rodriguez, who was sitting with his girlfriend and their two-year-old son, wept at the news. So did his girlfriend. Their son, too young to understand, simply said, as he departed with his mother at the end of the consultation, "Take care of my daddy!"

Bederson was visibly shaken after the encounter.

"I always try to retain whatever hope," he says. "Many of the young doctors today are so brutally honest—talking about the 'statistical likelihood' of survival. And I just don't get that. In Europe they don't tell. It's a cultural thing. They protect patients from unhappiness and sadness. After all, we're here to alleviate pain and suffering. But at the same time, ours is a society that's transparent. We share information. It's a real moral dilemma. And a balancing act."

Bederson says that neurosurgical training does not teach residents how to break terrible news to patients and family. "I can't tell my residents how to do it," he explains. "I lead by example. People need hope. A small percentage *do* get better." That Bederson feared the worst for Rodriguez, however, is clear as he evokes the patient's youth, his sweetly polite personality, his loving girlfriend, and his two-year-old son. "It's the strangest thing," he says. "The people with malignant brain tumors are always *nice*. When a guy comes in with a wife and a beautiful baby, you know it's going to be bad."

Challenging the notion that the best neurosurgeons are clinical, unemotional technicians, Bederson insists that it is crucial for brain surgeons to feel the horror and sadness that arise from cases like Rodriguez's.

"If you don't feel it, then you're too detached," he says. "The healer part is important. The thing is, neurosurgery is so difficult, there are so many details and complications, that you'll lose a sense of ownership of the patient if you don't feel the emotions of it." Bederson admits that some of the greatest neurosurgeons in history seemed to evince little empathy for their patients. Harvey Cushing was a famous tyrant and prima donna, and Charlie Wilson, for all his technical brilliance, has often been accused, by his former residents and colleagues, of a lack of caring for patients. One prominent neurosurgeon who trained under Wilson once told Bederson: "I'd have steady hands too, if I didn't give a fuck about the patient."

"There was a sense that he could do anything, because if there was a bad outcome, it wouldn't faze him," Bederson says. Others insist that, although Wilson's bedside manner left much to be desired, he did empathize with patients. "I would often have to go around after Dr. Wilson had made rounds," says Robert Spetzler, the chief of neurosurgery at Barrow Neurological Institute in Phoenix and another Wilson trainee, "and quiet down the families, because he could be so abrupt and appear to be uncaring—although he cared deeply."

No such debate exists about the other most famous neurosurgeon of the twentieth century: Gazi Yaşargil was famous for the tortures he put himself through on behalf of patients, suffering bouts of insomnia before and after surgeries or breaking out in hives when he had a bad outcome. Bederson tries to steer a middle path between these two extremes—which is, he says, the only way to proceed in the specialty without becoming paralyzed by fear of harming his patients.

"To be a neurosurgeon," he says, "you have to have some sort of ego strength, maybe to the point of pathology, to think that you can drill holes in someone's head and help them. There's a saying: 'I need that like I need a hole in the head.' But as a neurosurgeon, you *believe* that you are doing *good* by drilling holes in someone's head. Almost by definition it means that you are either overconfident or you have, maybe, a too high opinion of yourself. Yet you need that. To do it. To drill the hole. You need that almost pathological self-belief. But if you don't apply some sort of humility, you're going to hurt people and you won't be a good neurosurgeon. So you need to combine this hubris with humility. And achieving that balance is not so easy.

"It's exhausting work and you can so easily miss a detail that can kill a patient," he goes on. "Before every operation now, I ask myself, 'How can I accidentally hurt this patient?' Every time. That comes from a horrible error I made one time. I didn't slow down. I was running two operating rooms, two cases, at the same time. I was preparing for a room upstairs and a room downstairs. I made a horrible mistake. I operated on the wrong side." He pauses, as if considering whether he wishes to say more about this. He does not. "We do five thousand cases a year now at Mount Sinai," he continues. "There is a significant error rate. And that's the human aspect of this. Unless you own the patient, you can't learn from errors. Unless you feel it in your gut, they are just a technical challenge."

Bederson holds a "Quality Assurance" meeting (formerly known as "Morbidity and Mortality") with the entire department, once a month, in which residents and attending surgeons discuss in detail the cases that developed "complications" over the previous four weeks. The point of the exercise, he says, is to not only improve outcomes by pointing up areas of weakness, but to force every neurosurgeon in the program to recognize his or her responsibility for the fate of each patient. Bederson himself has a small private ritual that he started performing before each operation after the grievous error he made by operating on the wrong side of the patient's head.

"You have to scrub before every case—to wash your hands," he says. "I use that time now to say, 'Remember, this is a human being.' I'm really not religious, but I say, 'God, please don't let me hurt this patient.' Because there is all this craziness in your day. The beeper going off. Phone calls. Budget meetings. If I can just find a moment to stop and say,

'Don't hurt this patient,' then I'm not thinking about all the other stuff. I focus."

FOCUS BECOMES AN ISSUE the next morning, when Bederson is scheduled to remove Rodriguez's malignant brain tumor. Because of the emergency scheduling of the procedure, Bederson's usual operating room, OR #2, is not available, and his staff has to scramble to find him an open room. None was available on the neurosurgery ward, so the team has had to improvise a room two floors below, in OR #8, a pediatric cardiology operating room. OR #8 has a completely different layout from the neurosurgery rooms and none of the necessary equipment—all of which has to be brought from upstairs. As members of the team hurry in and out of the room bearing pieces of equipment, Bederson, pacing in the hallway outside, casts a baleful glance at the flow of people rushing in and out, the double doors swinging wide onto the busy corridor. "That's a danger of infection, all these people going in and out," he says. But there's nothing to be done about it. Bederson retreats to his office.

By 9:30 a.m., the room is finally ready. Rodriguez, in a hospital gown and socks, is led in, on his own two feet, supported on either side by two residents, his gait unsteady, a strip of hair shaved from the nape of his neck to the crown, evidence of the operation a few weeks ago to place the VP shunt. He is helped onto the bed and put under. Bederson's chief resident, Mascitelli, opens the cranium, cutting a small square window on the left side of Rodriguez's head.

At 10:15 a.m., Bederson enters the OR where Mascitelli, the anesthesiologist, the scrub nurse, another nurse, and Schlacter have been waiting for him. All sense of the earlier chaos and confusion has been eliminated from the room: Rodriguez is draped, his cranium open, the microscope in place. The room lights have been turned down. The Brain Lab computer screens and the three overhead operating lights glow against the surrounding darkness.

"Beautiful!" Bederson says. "So pretty!"

He settles into the chair, takes up his instruments, and gets to work. He has not been operating long when he says, on a hopeful note, "Interesting. This might just be a low-grade glioma." Such tumors can be treated with surgery, radiation, and other drugs and are not the immediate death sentence that a high-grade glioma is.

"From your mouth to God's ears," Schlacter mutters.

A few minutes later, Bederson says to Mascitelli: "See those thrombosed blood vessels?" "Thrombosis" refers to blood clots, of the kind that can form in the presence of a tumor. Bederson points with his forceps at several clots, dark masses, in the large veins that squiggle through the tumor. "What does that make you think of?"

"Lymphoma?"

"Or possibly GBM," Bederson says. GBM: short for "glioblastoma multiforme." High-grade glioma. The worst possible diagnosis.

Schlacter, who has heard the ominous interchange, says quietly, "Oh . . ."

Bederson uses the bipolar forceps to pluck off a blobby sample of the tumor. He holds it out to the scrub nurse, who removes it with his gloved fingers. The sample is taken immediately to the pathology lab for a frozen analysis. Bederson continues removing the tumor, which is gray and slimy and looks like uncooked oyster on the half shell. He again raises the possibility that it is something other than a high-grade glioma. Perhaps, he says, it *is* a lymphoma, which is treatable with radiation and chemotherapy, and for which the prognosis is good if the patient is young, as Rodriguez is, and does not suffer from an immune system disease like AIDS, as Rodriguez does not.

At 11:05 a.m., the lab calls down with the frozen results. Mascitelli takes it. He listens for a moment. "Okay," he says into the phone. "Thank you." He hangs up. "High-grade glioma."

10

Neurosurgery residents eager to become academic surgeons at a teaching hospital usually delay entering practice, after their seven years of training, and add to their résumé by doing a series of fellowships to hone their surgical skills and deepen their knowledge of a particular subspecialty, whether it is brain tumors, spinal surgery, epilepsy surgery, vascular surgery.

Bederson, upon completing his residency at UCSF in 1990, secured one of the most coveted fellowships in all of neurosurgery: in Zurich with Gazi Yaşargil, the acknowledged father of modern microneurosurgery. Though sixty-five years old at the time, Yaşargil was, Bederson says, still at the height of his powers. "He was the world's greatest neurosurgeon of the twentieth century," Bederson says. "The greatest. Above Wilson. Pure genius. He was the Picasso of neurosurgery. They said about Picasso, who was Spanish and moved to Paris, that he was 'a savage born in a savage country transforming a civilized world.' Yaşargil was the same way. He was a Turk, educated in Turkey, and he came to Switzerland, the most buttoned-down place in the world. He had a similar lack of respect as Picasso for the way things were done. Bringing in the microscope. Inventing new approaches into the brain. Inventing new tools and instruments. He had an amazing sense of three-dimensional anatomy. I saw him clip aneurysms in a totally intuitive, rapid-fire way that was quite amazing. So fast. He could see things that no one else could see." Bederson was also struck by the stark contrast between Wilson's personal approach to patients and Yaşargil's, who "would kill himself if he had a bad outcome."

Bederson spent six months in Zurich with Yaşargil, focusing on vascular neurosurgery—the subspecialty that treats abnormalities of the blood vessels, including aneurysms and arteriovenous malformations, or AVMs, a congenital defect characterized by knotted bundles of arteries and veins that, because of their unusual anatomy, are at high risk for fatal clots and uncontrolled bleeding. "He put me in an office right next to his and I just spent every single day with him for six months," Bederson says. "He confided in me, he talked with me, he reviewed cases with me, we wrote a couple of papers together."

Bederson followed this with a final six-month fellowship, in cerebrovascular surgery, under Robert Spetzler at the Barrow Neurological Institute in Phoenix, Arizona—another coveted position. Though then only in his forties, Spetzler had already gained a worldwide reputation on a par with Wilson and Yaşargil. The 1997 book *The Healing Blade* recounts Spetzler's expertise in the so-called "standstill" technique for operating on aneurysms too dangerous to clip. Spetzler would lower the patient's body temperature, still the brain waves, and stop the heart for the duration of the operation, to prevent the chance of the aneurysm rupturing; he would seal it, then walk the patient back to life. Like Bederson, Spetzler had done his residency training under Wilson and was known to have been Wilson's prize trainee. For years after Spetzler had finished his residency at UCSF, Wilson would use Spetzler's brilliance to browbeat his trainees, saying, admonishingly, "That's not how Robert would do it."

"He's the modern-day surgical genius," Bederson says about Spetzler. "He takes Wilson and Yaşargil and rolls it all up into a highly competitive, athletic type of personality—great sense of humor, friendly, kind, *supremely* talented. As talented as Yaşargil. So he's like the whole package in a somewhat-normal-human-being."

For fellowship positions, Spetzler had his pick of the best

trainees in the world. "When you have a fellowship that everyone wants to get into," Spetzler says, "it's the incredible privilege of the fellowship director to pick the people whom you think have the greatest promise. And Josh was one of those. He had a hunger for learning, remarkable drive, and a quest for excellence."

Bederson says that the advantages conferred on him by training with the top three neurosurgeons of the last century (Wilson, Yaşargil, and Spetzler) cannot be overestimated. "Neurosurgery is *such* a hierarchical field that these years of training are as much like a duck imprinting as they can be," he says. "It defines you. Neurosurgeons from around the world will flock to hear great people talk, see great people operate. I guess, like art, you learn from the masters. So you learn something from a Spetzler or a Yaşargil or a Wilson that somehow synthesizes things in a way that other people haven't. There might be a certain genius that they apply in certain areas that other people don't have. You learn things that you just can't learn any other way."

Larry Pitts, who took over as chief of neurosurgery at UCSF after Wilson's retirement in 1999, concurs. "One of the most important features of seeing a technical master at work—either as a colleague or as a student—is that you suddenly see that something is *possible*," Pitts says. "You just weren't sure before. You'd never seen it done, so you didn't know. You see a technical master do it, and you suddenly know that it's possible and *you* might be able to do it too; and not only that, but you might apply the idea around a different corner and do something a little different. And that's how you move the specialty forward."

11

After completing his seven years of neurosurgery residency at UCSF and another year in post-doctoral training with Yaşargil and Spetzler, Bederson landed his first full-time job, as a junior attending neurosurgeon, at the age of thirty-four, at Montefiore Hospital, in the Bronx. It was not his first choice. Montefiore's neurosurgery department was ranked well below the places where he had trained, but he accepted the position as a compromise. He needed to find a hospital where his wife, Isabelle, could complete her neurosurgery residency.

The two had met at UCSF when he was in his third year of medical school, Isabelle in her first. "She comes from a very old family, in the north of Italy, of doctors and scholars," Bederson says. "She was a neurosurgeon in Turin and she knew she couldn't get trained properly there, so she got a brain tumor grant, took it to San Francisco, and happened to get a job in the same lab where I was. I courted the hell out of her and we eventually, *crazily*, decided to get married before she found out where she would be doing her neuro-surgery residency. We got married when I was a first-year resident."

Until that time, candidates for a neurosurgery residency were handpicked by the head of the department. But the year that Isabelle applied for her residency happened to be the year that all surgical specialties changed to the cur-rent recruiting method: the National Resident Matching Program, known as "the Match." Medical students rank their top choices, and the programs rank their top choice of students; the data are fed into a computer, and the result-ing match between student and program is arrived at by a double blind. That Isabelle would match at UCSF seemed statistically unlikely. But "miracle of miracles," Bederson says, "Isabelle matched at UCSF."

This should have been a cause for celebration. But Isabelle and Charlie Wilson were not a good match. "I could have stayed at UCSF as an attending surgeon—and I wanted to," Bederson says. "But I had to find a job where Isabelle could finish her residency and where it would be likely that she could find a position in the same city as me."

That proved to be Montefiore Medical Center, in the Bronx. "My consolation prize for living in the Bronx was that I got to take flying lessons," Bederson says. He bought a Piper Archer four-seater plane from a pathologist friend. "I flew out of White Plains airport," he says. "Got my instrument rating and went all over the place." As with so many of his hobbies, Bederson sees a direct connection between his passion for flying and neurosurgery—particularly the fine surgical art of operating when swirling blood or obscuring tissue hides his direct view of the lesion he is operating on, and he must rely on a combination of accrued anatomical knowledge and computer navigation. "That's very similar to those times, as a pilot, when heavy clouds completely obscure your vision and you're flying on instruments," he says. "I had some amazing flights up and down the St. Lawrence River in snow, flying on instrumentation alone, and eventually landing three hours later, coming out of the clouds. There are real parallels with brain surgery." (Isabelle, however, put her foot down about his flying when the couple had their first child in 1994. "She made him return the airplane that he bought," says his mother, Betty. "She told him, 'You're a father now, this will not do.'")

Bederson had been at Montefiore for only a few months when he received an invitation to join Mount Sinai as an attending surgeon. Mount Sinai's neurosurgery department had a storied past as the place where Dr. Leonard Malis (who helped Yaşargil pioneer the intra-operative microscope) had once been chief. Furthermore, Mount Sinai had just hired a new chief, Dr. Post, the former vice chairman at Columbia, one of the top-rated programs. There was buzz about Post hoping to build the department by hiring the best attending surgeons in the country. "It was a tremendous honor to be invited to join Mount Sinai," Bederson says. He joined the neurosurgery department in 1992.

Bederson was made director of Mount Sinai's cerebro-vascular program, specializing in aneurysms and AVMs. He also obtained a large NIH grant and launched Mount Sinai's first neurosurgical basic science lab, studying stroke and subarachnoid hemorrhage—bleeding between the ce-rebral cortex and the membrane that encases the brain. But he soon shifted away from vascular surgery, as technological innovations rendered his expertise in that area increasingly obsolete. Today, clipping aneurysms has for the most part been replaced by a procedure called "endovascular coiling," in which surgeons cut a small incision on the inside of the thigh and introduce a thin wire catheter into the femoral artery. They feed the catheter through the blood vessels, up the body, and into the brain, where a platinum coil on the end of the catheter is inserted into the aneurysm and expanded, to block the blood flow and eliminate the pos-sibility of rupture. The coil is left inside the aneurysm as a permanent way to prevent it from again filling with blood. The FDA approved the process in 1995, three years after Bederson joined Mount Sinai. Rather than retrain in this type of surgery, Bederson shifted to his other great area of expertise: the surgical removal of skull-base tumors, those that grow close to the bottom of the skull, where a number of critical blood vessels and nerves are located (as in the operation on Robert O'Shea), or close to the top of the skull behind the eye and forehead.

By 2007, after fifteen years at Mount Sinai, Bederson, about to turn fifty, was growing restless—and ambitious. He wanted to be chief of his own neurosurgery department, and he made no secret of his ambitions to his bosses at Mount Sinai. Dr. Post was turning sixty-five and felt ready to step down as chief—on condition that he be allowed to continue in the department as an attending surgeon.

"I'd been chair for eighteen years," Post says. "I was tired of the administrative stuff. I thought I'd built the department into a really great *clinical* department, and now I was thinking it was time to build the science side—and that wasn't my strength. I thought Josh might be able to build the laboratories. He had a research grant and he had a lab going. I spoke to the dean of the medical school, Dennis Charney, and the CEO, Kenneth Davis, and said I thought Josh was an excellent candidate to replace me as chief. I told them that Josh had been interviewing to be chair at various places, including Cleveland Clinic and at Pittsburgh. I said, 'He's got great potential, why have him leave?'"

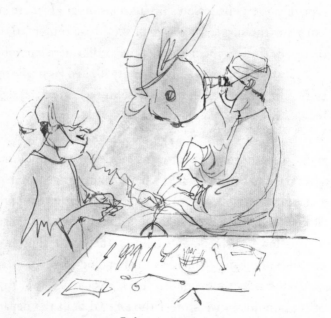

Bederson operating

Charney and Davis agreed—and in 2007, Bederson became chief of neurosurgery at Mount Sinai. At the time, the department ranked only in the midfifties, out of the country's roughly one hundred neurosurgery programs, in *U.S. News & World Report*'s annual list of the country's best neurosurgery departments. The rankings are based on criteria that include the number of "high risk" patients treated, their survival rate, the advanced technologies available, and reputation among specialists in the field. Bederson set out to improve the department in all areas. "I wanted to make us a superpower," he says.

"I traveled and learned models of other departments around the country," he says. "I believed our department should be more than an amalgam of what we call 'service lines': pituitary tumors, pediatric neurosurgery, spine surgery, trauma, movement disorders, skull base tumors, neurocritical care. I felt that each of these service lines should be treated like its own department. Each one should have a famous leader, someone top in the field. The only way to achieve that was to grow the department. But how? To make it as a neurosurgeon, you need to do two hundred surgeries a year—and that's why, traditionally, neurosurgeons do all these different kinds of surgery, because otherwise there are just not enough cases. Neurosurgical problems are actually relatively rare. So if I was going to move from a general neurosurgery mentality to this superspecialty model, we would have to have *more* cases, so that our attending surgeons could concentrate on their specialty and still have enough work. We had to reach out to compete, to take cases from NYU and Columbia and all the other neurosurgery programs in the New York area—and beyond. So the vision was strategic, political, monetary. I had to learn a different language. And I was helped because the leadership of the hospital merged with Continuum Health Partners. In one day in 2013, we added five hospitals to the Mount Sinai system, including Beth Israel and St. Luke's Roosevelt and Mount Sinai Eye and Ear—and all of them could now refer neurosurgery cases to us."

When Post took over as chief in the early 1990s, Mount Sinai did around 500 cases a year. Post grew that to 2,000 cases before he stepped down. Bederson has since raised the volume to over 5,000 annually, and he has added staff accordingly. "Today, we're the biggest program in New York City," he says. "By far. We are significantly bigger than Cornell, Columbia, NYU, Montefiore. Significantly."

The department's track record for patient survival, the volume of "high-risk" surgeries (like the one on O'Shea), the aggressive hiring of leading specialists, and Bederson's commitment to making the department a leader in advanced technology (to say nothing of the subtle but real status conferred by Bederson's reputation and pedigree) have lifted Mount Sinai to a current rank of twelfth in *U.S. News*. This is still well below the top three (Mayo Clinic, Johns Hopkins, and New York-Presbyterian) and several notches below UCSF (which has fallen to fifth place from its number one ranking when Charlie Wilson was in charge), but the department's fast rise from what Bederson calls a "no show" rank to the brink of the top ten has put Mount Sinai on the lips of every neurosurgeon in the country and has enabled Bederson to attract top attending surgeons, thus growing the department and increasing the volume of surgeries, fueling his drive to take Mount Sinai to the top of the rankings. "I'm determined to make this department as good as the places where *I* trained," he says.

The dramatically improved ranking has also made the department a magnet for the best and brightest medical students seeking a neurosurgery residency.

"Last year we had 310 applications for the two spots in our program," Bederson says. "Which raises the question: How does one even *attempt* to choose two people out of that many? We have a committee that looks at their CVs and scores. But we want to take the whole person into account. So after we've winnowed the applicants down to forty-five, we meet with them, fifteen a day over three days. The whole department shuts down, we pair ourselves up, and we interview them. Have dinner with them. Some will come back and spend another day or two with us. And it's not only the top people from Ivy League schools that we want."

Bederson cites as an example a current fourth-year resident, Eric Oermann, a graduate of Georgetown University who, in 2015, during his third year as a resident, was named to the *Forbes* "30 Under 30" list of the nation's leading health care innovators for research he did on predicting survival rates for patients with advanced Stage IV cancers. "When you meet cancer patients, the one thing that *everyone* wants to know is, How much longer do I have to live?" says Oermann, a slightly built man with wire-rimmed spectacles and an intensely cerebral manner. "And the honest answer is, we can do little better than flip a coin. So my interest was to try to build a model to try to predict survival." Trained as an undergraduate in artificial intelligence and the use of so-called "machine learning"—the teaching of computers to perform tasks without being explicitly programmed—Oermann used the existing data about mortality rates to arrive at more accurate survival predictions for cancer patients. His work has real-world application on hospital wards. "This way, we can better help patients decide what kind of care and treatment they want—whether it's palliative care to reduce pain and suffering, or more aggressive treatments to try to extend life." Astonishingly, Oermann managed to conduct his groundbreaking research while completing his first two years in the residency program. "Didn't sleep a lot," he says, laughing. "I've found I'm fairly tolerant to sleep deprivation. If I get four hours, I can function pretty well. Which isn't that uncommon in neurosurgery."

Oermann recently agreed to take a two-year hiatus from his neurosurgery residency to move to California and work at Google, which had learned of his work in machine learning, an area into which the search engine company has been rapidly expanding. The offer also gives Oermann the opportunity to reunite with his wife, an oncologist who trained at Mount Sinai and is currently doing cancer research at Stanford University. "I don't actually know *what* I'll be doing with Google yet," he says. "They just hired me. We'll see!" He expects, in any case, to keep his hand in as a neurosurgeon. "I don't think I could go two years without operating," he says. "I really do enjoy it. I'll come back to Mount Sinai and scrub with Dr. Bederson once in a while— or I know a lot of the guys in California, at UCSF and Stanford. I might see them and say, 'Hey, can I join you for a few days?' All these guys know each other in multiple ways: They'll have trained with someone or they'll have studied under the same people or done projects together, because it's one of the smallest specialties in medicine. There's a real community feel."

Not all residents in the Mount Sinai program project Oermann's focused, brainy intensity—at least, not on the surface. Robby Rothrock, a second-year resident, is known by his colleagues for his casual, seemingly laid-back manner—a breezy, self-assured confidence that, as Schlacter puts it, "borders on cocky." Tall and athletic looking, with the finely chiseled features of an actor and thick black hair that he often hides beneath a colored bandanna, Rothrock grew up in Miami. "I always had the gift of gab," he says. "I was a thespian in high school, I did all the plays, everybody thought I would be an actor—or a lawyer. I never thought I'd end up as a scientist or physician." But two things happened, he says, during his freshman year at U Penn, where he majored in intellectual history. "One, I met all the other kids who wanted to be lawyers. *That* was a real social conversion—seeing all these sycophants who just wanted to make a lot of money." The other thing that happened was a freak accident suffered by his uncle's friend, who fell down the stairs in his house and sustained a C-3 fracture—a break in the third cervical vertebra in the neck, which can be fatal.

"He was rushed to hospital and had an emergency decompression and spinal fusion," Rothrock says. "Two neurosurgeons saved his life. I was hating pre-law, and neurosurgery seemed like this noble-seeming profession. I came home and said, 'I want to be a neurosurgeon.' I was nineteen. My mom tried to call my bluff and forced me to spend my summer working as a medical assistant at a family friend's practice. I worked in a general practitioner's office and volunteered in an emergency department, shadowing an orthopedic surgeon and a neurosurgeon. To my mom's dismay, I loved it."

Rothrock completed his major in intellectual history while taking makeup courses in the prerequisites for medical school—biology, chemistry, organic chemistry, and physics—during summer sessions. He also worked in an animal lab dissecting rodents. "I got into four medical schools," he says, "and chose Einstein in Philadelphia." When it came time to apply to neurosurgery residency programs, he put Mount Sinai in his top five. Applicants register for the Match in mid-September of their final year of medical school and learn where they matched in mid-March—a grueling seven-month wait. "The Match process is unique," he says, with dry understatement. "You're contractually obligated to go wherever the system says. If you drop out, you're ineligible to participate again. So it's crazy. Waiting to find out where you matched is incredibly stressful. Not knowing where you're going to go—whether Texas or L.A., or back to Miami. If you even get in anywhere."

Now finishing his second year at Mount Sinai, he says that neurosurgery is, so far, everything he had hoped it would be.

"I think most of us are drawn to the difficulty," he says. "But it also has to do with the patient population. Brain tumor patients are a great example of 'Why do bad things happen to good people?' They're some of the nicest people—it's bizarre. I was somewhat drawn to that. There's a certain element of being able to help someone. It changes their life. That's a big thing. It's something that I don't know I would have gotten out of practicing law, or if I'd gone into plastics, doing breast surgery."

At the same time, Rothrock has made some unexpected discoveries about himself. Given his easy social manner, he at first thought that his greatest strengths as a resident would be interactions with patients, colleagues, and nurses. Instead, this is where he struggles the most, he says. "I always thought of myself as a great people person—but most of my issues have been with being impatient with other services or being impatient with patients themselves." Bederson, however, thinks that Rothrock judges himself so harshly in this area precisely because it *is* a strength. "I actually think he is superb at that—the interpersonal interactions, which are very important in neurosurgery," Bederson says. "I think he's the best of all the residents at that. It's just that he *cares* about it." As a second-year resident, Rothrock is not yet allowed to remove tumors, but his skill at sewing up incisions and other rudiments of surgery have shown that he has high potential as a surgeon: good hand-eye coordination, fluidity, and speed. "The technical stuff—which I never expected to be particularly great at—has been good," Rothrock says. "I think the quality of stuff I do, surprisingly, is not bad: in terms of how the incision looks at the end, how eloquently you move your hands." Bederson concurs. "He's good," he says. "He's going to be a spectacular surgeon."

No resident, however, is excellent in every facet of the training.

"It's my job as a leader to identify their strengths," Bederson says. "And I also ask: 'Where are they weak?' And then I push the *hell* out of them." He can be a stern taskmaster and a sharp-eyed, sharp-tongued critic. One day, while placing a VP shunt, Bederson noted that the sixth-year resident was fumbling as he tried to insert the flexible tube into the rigid irrigation rod. "What are you *doing*?" he snapped. "Your *angle* is wrong!" On another day, during neuroradiology rounds, he close-questioned a third-year resident, in front of the whole department, about a certain part of the brain's anatomy. When the resident failed to answer correctly, Bederson asked him to go up to one of the large computer displays mounted on the wall and point out the structure on the patient's MRI. The resident went up to the screen but merely stood there, helplessly. When he moved to sit down, Bederson said, "The pain isn't over yet," and he proceeded to ask more questions that the man was unable to answer. The resident was finally allowed to resume his seat. Later, Bederson asked a colleague if his grilling had been "too painful." "No," the colleague assured him, "he's *got* to learn the anatomy." "Yeah," Bederson agreed. "But it was painful for *me*."

Unlike his former mentor Charlie Wilson, Bederson is slow to fire residents. "I make a commitment to these people," he says. "These are *already* the top of the cream of the top of the cream. So once I make a commitment, they're going to get through." Still, some residents do struggle to a degree that can imperil their chances of graduating. Last July, one of Bederson's residents was having trouble mastering the technical side of surgery. He described the resident as "smart, compassionate, nice, good communication," but "not a good surgeon." He expressed some doubts about whether the resident would graduate.

Signs of this resident's discomfort in the OR were obvious one day when the resident was scheduled to assist Bederson in the clipping of an aneurysm that could not be operated on with the less dangerous endovascular coiling. While preparing the patient, the resident seemed awkward and self-conscious, bumping the small instrument tray with a hand, accidentally dropping a suction tool when lifting it. When Bederson took over to clip the aneurysm, he pointedly demonstrated the most basic rudiments of surgery, including how to sit in the chair. "Find the most ergonomic position possible," he said. "Back straight. Know where your heels and toes are. Arms on the rest at about 90 degrees, where they're comfortable enough that you can sit barely moving for three or four hours."

Throughout the operation, Bederson narrated, in uncharacteristic detail, his every move. "This is the anterior choroidal artery," he said as he cleared a pathway toward the aneurysm. "It's very small but unforgiving. It supplies an area of the brain that contains cabling for motor function. If you occlude it, they don't walk again. This white structure here that's very soft—it's the ocular motor nerve that opens and closes the eye and moves it. If you damage that nerve, she's as good as blind."

At one point, he allowed the resident to take up the instruments and advance into the Sylvian fissure. "When you introduce your instruments, you want to decrease the magnification on the scope," he said. "Advance your sucker. Less thumb. Even less. Slip past the temporal lobe. Okay, the bipolar is in your right hand . . . Little too much thumb . . ."

Bederson admits that you can judge a resident too quickly. Sometimes people who show little promise early on unexpectedly blossom. Amir Madani, the resident with whom Bederson removed the frontal lobe tumor lining back in early June, was on the brink of being let go early in his training. Which is why Bederson still holds out hope for his current struggling resident. Three more months of training could make the difference. Ultimately, he says, he thinks this resident is going to be fine. "Same with Amir," he adds. "I knew he was going to make it."

12

Two days after Henry Rodriguez underwent surgical removal of his malignant brain tumor, he is able to return home to his girlfriend and son. Four days after that, he comes back to Mount Sinai for a post-op follow-up. He arrives at the small suite of offices adjoining Bederson's inner sanctum a little after nine o'clock. He is alone, dressed in light colored jeans stylishly sagging, a long-sleeved t-shirt, a white baseball cap bearing an American flag, and pristine new Nike basketball shoes. He is scheduled, later that day, to meet a landlord about a new apartment, into which he and his girlfriend are hoping to move because it has a small bedroom for their son.

Schlacter, who often pre-interviews patients for Bederson, greets Rodriguez with a cheerful "Hi!" at the door to the suite, hugs him, and then asks him to walk across the room so that she can check his balance. He moves slowly, lifting his feet carefully, like someone trying to pass a sobriety test under the gaze of a watchful cop. After five or six steps, he veers slightly into the wall.

"Hey, you walked into my wall," Schlacter says, in a lightly teasing tone.

"That's just because I'm anxious," he says.

Schlacter brings him into her small office, closes the door, and asks him to sit in the chair opposite her desk. She draws her chair up in front of his.

"Pucker your lips," she says, scrutinizing his mouth closely. "Stick out your tongue. Move it side to side. Show me your teeth." He moves his mouth sluggishly. "Does that feel weird for you?" she asks.

"Um, yeah," he says. "It curls up right here." He points to the right side of his mouth.

"Yup," Schlacter says. "The right side is still weak."

There is a brief knock on the door, and Bederson, dressed in his surgical greens, comes into the room. He shuts the door behind him, smiles warmly at Rodriguez, then takes a seat on a small sofa to Rodriguez's right.

"So," Bederson says, "how are you feeling?"

"He's still got some numbness," Schlacter says.

"How about the headaches?" Bederson asks.

"Mild," says Rodriguez.

Bederson nods for a moment, takes in a deep breath, and looks Rodriguez in the eye. All vestiges of a smile are gone from Bederson's face.

"Well," he begins, in a quiet, steady voice, "we have to start treating this. Do you remember how we talked about how things in the brain are not either black or white? Benign or malignant? There are shades. This one is not on the benign side, for sure. It is not cured by the surgery that I did." He explains that preliminary findings from the more detailed pathology analysis suggest that the tumor is not, as initially feared from the frozen sample, the most malignant of all—a glioblastoma multiforme. "It's somewhere in this gray shade," Bederson continues. "Between them."

In fact, the pathology report suggests that Rodriguez is suffering from an anaplastic ependymoma grade III, a rare form of malignant cancer that originates in the cells that line the ventricles of the brain and the center of the spinal cord. This is not an immediate death sentence, but it is serious in the extreme: Patients have a survival rate of less than 65 percent and a life expectancy, at the low end, of five years, and at the high end, of eighteen. Highly malignant and invasive, the cancer has a tendency to grow back after treatment, and to invade healthy brain tissue aggressively. And some chance still exists that Rodriguez is suffering from the more fatal form of cancer—the final verdict will not be known until the pathology lab has done a still more detailed analysis. Bederson, however, keeps all of this to himself, preferring instead to accentuate the positive: the existence of new drugs that have shown promise in beating back the tumor's growth; and new radiation therapy, known as stereotactic radio surgery, which uses a thin beam to focus directly on a tumor, to attack it with greater efficacy than older forms of radiation that dangerously bombard large parts of the brain.

"The good news is that some patients have an incredible response to the new drugs," Bederson says. "It's not a high percentage, but there are some who are cured—completely cured—by the treatments."

"How many treatments?" Rodriguez asks quietly. "Six? Eight?"

"You know all this?" Bederson says, in a slightly admonishing tone. "You've read about it already?" He had, some weeks ago, urged Rodriguez to stay off the Internet.

"Just a little bit," Rodriguez says, on a note of apology. "I mean, I try to stay away from the negative . . ."

"Well, it's still bad to Google, because if you look up 'malignant brain tumor' you're going to see all kinds of things that would be very scary. If there's one thing that I'd like you to come away with today, it's the following. Two pieces of good in all this: Even in the ones that are the worst, there is an increasing, and significant, *superb* response rate to the treatments. People will go for years and years with a super-high quality of life. We've seen decades of survival, even in the worst ones, okay? So, hopefully, you're going to be one of those. And a young age is the most important factor that predicts a really good outcome. So, even if it turns out that it's worse than I think it is, there's *still* reason for hope. Okay? That's number one. Number two, I don't *think* it's that really bad one. Based on what I've seen so far, it falls much more in the gray zone."

Rodriguez asks a number of questions—practical questions—about where the treatments would be administered, how long he would have to take off work, what side effects he might expect. Bederson answers each in detail. Then both men fall silent, as if suddenly aware of some huge unspoken reality that they have not touched on, cannot touch on. They are looking at each other—a silent ten seconds of unbroken eye contact. A high-pitched noise comes from the back of Rodriguez's throat, a throttled sob, a helpless moan of pain and grief and fear.

"What are you going to do?" Bederson says softly. "It's a hard diagnosis to get. But don't give up hope. I'm not fooling when I say we have a lot of good responders."

Rodriguez sucks in breath. Steadies himself. "I've come this far . . . so . . ."

"That's right," Bederson says. "That's right. And you've got a long way to go."

"I *hope* so," Rodriguez says. "For my sake. My girlfriend's sake. My *son's* sake."

"Yeah," Bederson says, almost in a whisper. "That's right. That's right. I'm with you on that."

13

All of medicine, but perhaps neurosurgery especially—given its intimate connection to the deepest mysteries of identity and consciousness and everything that makes us human—acquaints its patients and practitioners with the highs and lows of despair and hope, illness and health, life and death.

Bederson's next patient is a woman in her early forties, a cherubic, broadly smiling African-American woman who immediately disperses the heavy aura of gloom that had filled Schlacter's office like a cloud.

"Hello, hello!" the woman cries.

Schlacter jumps up from her desk and embraces her. "So good to see you!"

The woman sits. An infectious joy and vitality seems to emanate from her, like a physical glow, as if she feels a stronger delight in life than ordinary people and cannot help but communicate this, infectiously, through her beaming smile, her whooping laughter. It is no illusion. This is the woman from whom Bederson and Madani had removed the left frontal lobe tumor, rescuing her from over two decades of depression, completely transforming her personality, filling her with a euphoric optimism that feels, to everyone around her, nearly palpable. Having settled on the sofa, she talks to Schlacter about this transformation—or, more accurately, "restoration," since she has not, in her own mind, *changed*. She has gone back to someone she had been long ago.

"It's like . . . like . . . a *return*," she says, describing how she had emerged from the darkness and self-loathing that had engulfed her for so long. "Because I remember, now, when I was fifteen, sixteen—I loved myself. I had a mirror. I used to kiss the mirror!" She lets out one of her whooping laughs. "I'm forty years old, but I feel like I'm that age again! How can I say it? I feel like I'm *young*."

As a child and teenager, she had been filled with optimism and energy, attending gifted classes in high school and planning to go into fashion design. "High school was the best," she says. "I loved it. Rode the subway alone for the first time. I was thirteen. I loved the experience in that school." She cannot pinpoint when the darkness began to descend. It was a stealthy onset, as slow and inexorable as the tumor's growth in her head—a growth that might have begun as early as her infancy, with the mutant splitting of a single cell, acting under an abnormal genetic instruction.

Then dividing again. And again. All she knows is that, by the time she was in freshman year in college, something in her outlook had drastically changed. The spark, the joy, had gone out of her. Or almost. That was the year she met and fell in love with the man who would become her husband. But by the time they married a year later, something had gone badly wrong. "I wore a black dress at my wedding," she says. "I can't explain it. I just did. I felt like my life was ending."

The birth of her first child offered no respite. "I've never told anyone this," she says. "For five days after she was born, I didn't hold her." A few years later, a second child was born, a son. She didn't touch him either. She withdrew from life. Gone were any dreams of a career in fashion or anything else. "I used to wake up and sit in one chair all day, watching TV. At my kids' school they would ask my husband, 'Why doesn't your wife say hi?' Or, 'She acts like I did something to her.' And my husband would just say, 'Well, that's just how she is.' He got hurt a lot by me being so noncommunicative. Not being a wife. Luckily, he didn't go out and cheat. He's always been there. I don't know how he did it."

Only in retrospect can she recall odd symptoms that might have pointed to the tumor slowly growing in her frontal lobe. Bouts of weakness on her right side. Headaches on the left side of her head. The vision blurring in her left eye. "But only for a minute or two and then it would go away. The eye doctor didn't see anything. So I would forget about it." Then came the car accident, six months ago, that gave her whiplash. Clipped by a pickup that tried to swerve around her at a red light. She suffered terrible pain in her neck and back. Then she began, inexplicably, to fall down. "I would get up from sitting—and fall. Or walking. Suddenly fall."

Her husband insisted she seek medical help. She was not interested, simply didn't *care* enough about her health. She hadn't been to the gynecologist in seven years. Sometime before, she'd found a lump in her breast—and had not bothered to have it looked at by a doctor. (Later, it turned out to be benign.) But under her husband's urging, she finally agreed to get physiotherapy for her neck pain. "And," she says, "the therapy person said, 'Let's take an MRI of your neck and back.' And it was in that MRI that they found the tumor." Her emotional responses were so deadened, she felt no fear, experienced no panic. "I just thought, 'Okay, it's there, in my brain.'"

She was referred to a local neurologist, who took one look at her MRI and saw a tumor so big that it seemed, by all rights, she should not be alive.

"The doctor looked so scared. I'll never forget his face. But I didn't care. It didn't matter to me."

Indeed, when she got home from the doctor's office, she didn't bother to Google the word *ganglioglioma*, which the doctor had told her was the type of tumor in her head. "I didn't do any research. My husband did that." He also insisted that she get the tumor removed, right away. "He said, 'We're going to go to New York. We're going to find the best doctor.' He stayed up until four a.m. looking on the Internet for the best neurosurgeon in New York. He found Dr. Bederson. And in the morning, he phoned. He spoke to *you*."

"Yup," says Schlacter. "And I remember when he emailed the scans of your tumor. I couldn't believe you were alive. I said to your husband, 'Can she come *today*?' He said you were out of state and that you'd fly here over the weekend and you'd be here Monday."

Her first surgery, to decompress the mass, was scheduled for first thing Monday morning. She felt no fear, no anxiety. She did happen to notice, before going under, the cap worn by the anesthesiologist, as he bent over her to put the IV needle in her arm. "His hat was yellow—and yellow is my favorite color. He was a young Asian guy. And he was the first person I saw when I woke up from the operation. And everything was different. I was so happy! I said to him, '*I know you!*'"

"So what did happiness *feel* like?" Schlacter asks. "How did you feel different from before?"

She frowns, wrestling with this epistemological conundrum. There are no words for it. No words for a feeling that changed everything. But suddenly the future opened up in front of her. And it was full of potentially beautiful things. Gone was the lethargy and depression that had pinned her to the sofa all day. When she got home after the first tumor decompression, she started exercising. Walking. For miles. "I went to a nutritionist. I lost over fifty pounds in three months. No salt. No fried foods. No rice. No wine. And I didn't miss them at all!" But the biggest changes were in regard to her family. Her children. Her husband. She cannot describe the love that flooded her heart at her first sight of them after the operation. She has not been able to stop hugging them, touching them, kissing them.

Her children, in particular, have had to make an adjustment to this "new" person. It has been harder on them than she had anticipated. Her daughter, especially, is confused by the overwhelming love expressed by someone who had never before displayed those emotions. "They're not used to it, and they find it awkward. All they've known is that 'other person,' as I call it. I wish I could go back in time and be who I am *now* for all their growing up. But I can't do that. That's a little bit hard. And my husband. I wish I could change everything that happened. I'm going to look for a support group for them, so that people can get used to who

I am. I don't have a problem with *myself*. But they have to get used to who I am. *I'm* not going to change. I'm looking forward to a *lot* of things. I'm going to do more exercise—not just walking. I'm going to go back to school and get a career out of nursing. I can't wait for those things. I just can't wait."

There is a knock at the door. Bederson, dressed in his surgical blues, a paper face mask hanging loose from around his neck, enters the office. "Well, you're looking *great!*" he says, beaming.

"Thanks to *you!*"

He deflects this, telling her that he had studied the most recent set of follow-up brain scans. They showed that there was no tumor left in her brain. "We got it all," he says.

"Is there a chance it will come back?" she asks.

"Very low chance," he says. "We do have to watch it. We'll follow it very closely. It's a low-grade tumor."

Bederson lingers for a few minutes, standing and leaning against a set of file cabinets, chatting, smiling as he listens to his patient talk about her mysterious and wonderful return to life. His phone vibrates in his pocket. He checks it—and politely excuses himself.

They are ready for him in OR #2.

Acknowledgments

I'd like to thank Jonathan Karp, president and publisher of Simon & Schuster, for asking if I'd be interested in writing some books in a proposed series about "becoming." This subject matter was especially congenial to me at the time since I had a son starting his freshman year of college and I was already pondering the mystery of how young people settle on what they hope to do, and *be*, for the rest of their lives. It also happens that I was, myself, thinking about new directions in which to take my life and writing and was thus aware that the process of change and *becoming* never really ends, even for someone rounding on his sixth decade.

A huge shout-out to my editor, Karyn Marcus, for always sounding interested, amused, curious, on the other end of the phone. Plus, she's the kind of editor who, when she returns your draft with a set of brilliant cuts and suggestions, indicates in the margin places where her tear ducts became activated (the places where I, too, did a lot of throat clearing and eye blinking as I wrote).

Thanks to Bob Castillo for his impeccable copy edit and for keeping track of the various narrative time-shifts (he suggested a crucial switch in tense from past to present in the book's final section).

A forceful thank-you to my eldest brother, Ted, a neurosurgeon, whose talk of subarachnoid hemorrhages and aneurysms over the decades gave me the illusion that I actually knew something about this incredible medical specialty—and who, when I called him at his home in Denver to ask if he knew of any neurosurgery centers for me to approach in my hometown of New York, said, "Well, Mount Sinai has been getting a lot of buzz . . ." Ted was also a great sounding board during my reporting and writing—although I must claim all errors as my own.

The secret to nonfiction writing of this kind is great access, and for that I can't thank Josh Bederson enough. He was amazingly generous with his time and was instrumental in arranging unfettered access to his residents, interns, patients, colleagues, and family (all of whom I also thank heartily). And a special thank-you to his physician's assistant, Leslie Schlacter. Her unfailing good spirits made this book, for all its journeying into some of the darkest moments in existence, a pleasure.

I thank my agent, Lisa Bankoff, who for years had been urging me to give Jonathan Karp a call.

Finally, thanks to my wife, Donna Mehalko—and not only for her usual forbearance while I tussled with the reporting and writing. After more than thirty years of working within a few feet of each other (she as an artist-illustrator, I as a writer), we have *finally* collaborated on a project together, for which I thank everyone in the S&S art and design departments, and beyond.

APPENDIX I: HOW TO BECOME
A NEUROSURGEON

The path to a career as a neurosurgeon is long and arduous. The following five steps are the traditional route.

1. UNDERGRADUATE

Aspiring neurosurgeons must earn a bachelor's degree with pre-med prerequisites, which include a mix of sciences and liberal arts courses; one year each of chemistry, organic chemistry, biology, and physics (with lab courses in each); a year of English; and a year of calculus or another advanced math class, including statistics.

Most medical schools demand an undergraduate grade point average of 3.5 (or better) as well as a high score on the Medical College Admission Test (MCAT). The MCAT is a standardized, seven-and-a-half-hour multiple-choice exam that tests basic scientific knowledge, critical reasoning, and problem solving. Students prepare extensively for the MCAT. Like the SAT, there are many prep courses available, and the Association of American Medical Colleges (which administers the MCAT) offers sample tests on their website; in addition, there are an array of MCAT test preparation companies easily found online.

Medical schools have become increasingly competitive. Chances of getting into a good medical school (or, increasingly, *any* medical school) are improved by doing extracurricular work during undergrad, including activities like a job-shadowing program in a hospital, volunteering or community service in health-related fields, and having stellar recommendations and (it bears repeating) top grades.

2. MEDICAL SCHOOL

Medical school is a four-year-long program that results in a Doctor of Medicine degree (MD). The first two years are dedicated to course and lab work in the biological and natural sciences, including physiology, chemistry, medical ethics, and the art and practice of medicine. For the final two years, medical students move from the classroom onto the hospital wards for a series of three-month rotations in specialties that include internal medicine, general surgery, pediatrics, obstetrics and gynecology, and urology.

Third year is when most medical students decide what specialty they want to go into. Those still hoping to become neurosurgeons often take advanced classes in medical diagnostics, clinical research, surgical practice, and disease management.

As well as completing classes and rotations, medical school graduates must take and pass the United States Medical Licensing Examination test (USMLE). The USMLE is administered in three steps:

Step 1 is usually taken after the second year of medical school and is a one-day exam that tests for basic science knowledge and is divided into seven 60-minute blocks and administered in one eight-hour testing session.

Step 2 is usually taken during the fourth year of medical school and is usually divided into two separate exams that test medical knowledge, skills, and understanding of clinical science for patient care.

Step 3 is typically taken at the end of the first year of residency. A two-day exam, it assesses medical knowledge and understanding of biomedical and clinical science for managing patients.

Neurosurgery hopefuls apply for a residency training program through the National Residency Matching Program (NRMP). You increase the chances of being matched with the program of your choice by having outstanding medical school grades, excellent USMLE scores, published research, and superb letters of recommendation.

3. INTERNSHIP AND NEUROSURGICAL RESIDENCY PROGRAM
Neurosurgical residencies begin with an internship year that starts on July 1. The residency proper lasts a minimum of six years, and up to eight, during which residents observe operations by licensed neurosurgeons and are gradually given greater hands-on experience of surgery as they progress through the program, until the final year, when, as chief residents, they are entrusted to perform procedures like helping to remove tumors. There are neurosurgery subspecialties (for instance, pediatric, peripheral, and spine surgery) that require additional, focused training after or near the end of a residency.

4. BECOMING STATE-LICENSED AND BOARD-CERTIFIED
Neurosurgeons hoping to burnish their reputations and status often apply for licensing through their state's medical board; high achievers only need apply (applications include submitting

test scores and school transcripts). Many also apply for board certification through the American Board of Neurological Surgery. This requires taking, and passing, yet another exam.

5. CONTINUING EDUCATION

Continuing education is required for neurosurgeons to renew licensing and board certification. Neurosurgeons may choose to subspecialize in a field such as oncology, pediatric neurosurgery, or deep brain stimulation, and complete a fellowship in these subspecializations, which can take several more years of education.

APPENDIX II

The following titles are highly recommended as vivid evocations of the life of a neurosurgeon, including the training and the day-to-day pressures and pleasures of the specialty.

ADDITIONAL READING

Do No Harm: Stories of Life, Death and Brain Surgery (2014)
by Henry Marsh
An indispensable and expertly written memoir by recently retired British brain surgeon Marsh, who breaks the silence around the anxieties inherent in neurosurgery, including the pain and horror of accidentally "hurting" patients through error.

When the Air Hits Your Brain: Tales from Neurosurgery (1996)
by Frank Vertosick, Jr., M.D.
Another admirably direct memoir by an actual neurosurgeon, with good detail on the training and pressures of the job.

When Breath Becomes Air (2016)
by Paul Kalanithi

Still another memoir by a neurosurgeon—but with a tragic twist. Kalanithi was wrapping up his arduous ten-year-long training as a brain surgeon when he was diagnosed with stage IV lung cancer.

The Healing Blade: A Tale of Neurosurgery (1993)
by Edward J. Sylvester
Deep-saturation reporting by a science journalist who spent three years haunting the neurosurgery ward at one of the leading brain surgery centers in the USA, the Barrow Neurological Institute, in Phoenix, Arizona. It includes a profile of Barrow's former chief surgeon, the legendary Dr. Robert Spetzler.

Harvey Cushing: A Life in Surgery (2005)
by Michael Bliss
When this biography was initially published in 2005, it had been fifty years since the last full-length biography of the father of modern neurosurgery, the incomparable but tyrannical Harvey Cushing. It was worth the wait.

Something Hidden: A Biography of Wilder Penfield (1981)
by Jefferson Lewis
Excellent biography of the pioneering American-born, Montreal-based neurosurgeon, who was second only to Cushing in terms of brilliance, creativity, and influence on the field.

No Man Alone: A Neurosurgeon's Life (1977)
by Wilder Penfield
Completed shortly before Penfield's death, this autobiography is engrossing and often moving.

Saturday: A Novel (2005)
by Ian McEwan
This novel's first-person narrator, a London neurosurgeon, was the result of copious research by McEwan—and it shows. A confident, stylish, and authoritative evocation of the inner, and outer, lives of a brain surgeon.

BOOKS ABOUT THE BRAIN
Anyone interested in operating on the brain would do well to read up on this amazing, and still deeply mysterious, organ. Here are some fine books on the subject.

Mystery of the Mind: A Critical Study of Consciousness and the Human Brain (1975)
by Wilder Penfield

Minds Behind the Brain: A History of the Pioneers and Their Discoveries (2000)
by Stanley Finger
This book offers a survey of some 5,000 years of research on (and treatment of) the brain in the form of detailed profiles of historical figures whose work "dramatically changed the scientific or medical landscape."

The Brain Facts Book
For a good primer that will give you the basic facts, I recommend this short online book, which is available for free download from the website of the Society for Neuroscience at http://www.brainfacts.org/the-brain-facts-book.

Handbook of Neurosurgery, Eighth Edition (2016)
by Mark S. Greenberg

BOOKS ON MEDICINE AND SURGERY
To become a neurosurgeon, you must first get a medical degree, so here are a handful of classic texts about becoming, and being, a doctor. The insights are applicable across a wide range of specialties, including neurosurgery.

Complications: A Surgeon's Notes on an Imperfect Science (2002)
by Atul Gawande
Anything by Gawande on the subject of medicine and surgery is worth reading. That's especially true of this book and the following one.

Better: A Surgeon's Notes on Performance (2007)
by Atul Gawande

The House of God: A Novel (1978)
by Samuel Shem, M.D.
This classic piece of fiction (by an actual doctor) is now forty years old, but is still in print and is still being read by every new generation of medical student hopefuls. A satire in the *Catch-22* mold, it's very funny, but also deeply serious about the ferocious grind of medical training. The *Times* put it best in 2009, on the occasion of the book's thirtieth anniversary: "a raunchy, troubling and hilarious novel that turned into a cult phenomenon devoured by a legion of medical students, interns, residents and doctors."

ONLINE RESOURCES FOR APPLYING
TO MEDICAL SCHOOL

The Internet, of course, offers unending "expert" advice on how to apply to medical school, how to get into the best school, how to ace the MCAT, and so on. Here's a list of sites that are actually authoritative and useful.

Association of American Medical Colleges (AAMC). The AAMC is a nonprofit founded in 1876, and it administers the MCAT, the standardized test for med school admissions, so you can trust this website to steer you properly.
aamc.org/

American Medical Student Association (AMSA). This site tells you which undergrad premed courses to take, the dates for the MCAT, and résumé-polishing activities that make a difference to med schools. It has live links for each subject.
amsa.org/takes-get-medical-school/

Pre Med 101: Know What You Need to Get into Medical School. Informative, punchy, well-organized website with details about non-US schools, how to conduct yourself in a medical school in-

terview, whether to take AP courses in high school, and other salient topics.
medicalschoolhq.net/pre-med-101-everything-you-need-to-know -as-a-pre-med-student/

WikiHow. Sometimes a bullet-pointed website heavy on colorful graphics can help cut through the clutter and give you the main points clearly and quickly. WikiHow leads you by the hand through the steps for how to get into medical school.
http://www.wikihow.com/Get-Into-Medical-School

SDN (student doctor network). Nicely organized and user-friendly website on what you need to know about applying to medical school, residency, and related topics.
https://www.studentdoctor.net/

ONLINE RESOURCES FOR APPLYING FOR NEUROSURGICAL RESIDENCIES
Applying for neurosurgical residency is done through the National Resident Matching Program. Its website is an indispensable resource.
http://www.nrmp.org/

The American Association of Neurological Surgeons (AANS) is a scientific and educational association with 10,000 members worldwide. Its website says: "Find out what kinds of cases you will be seeing, what is covered in a neurosurgeon's training and what a neurosurgeon's life is like. Use this site as your first stop in learning about neurosurgery and as your portal to some of the best web resources."
http://www.aans.org/

The American Association of Neurological Surgeons maintains a website with excellent information about the Match, with good and clear advice about the application process, tests, grades, dates for submission of applications, and tips about letters of recommendation.
http://www.neurosurgerymatch.org/

ABOUT THE AUTHOR

John Colapinto is an award-winning journalist, author, and staff writer at the *New Yorker*. His nonfiction book, *As Nature Made Him: The Boy Who Was Raised as a Girl*, was a *New York Times* bestseller. He is the author of two novels, *About the Author* and *Undone*. He lives in New York City.